GENERALISSIMO
el BUSHO

ISBN 1-56163-384-4, clothbound edn.
ISBN 1-56163-385-2, paperback edn.
©2004 Ted Rall

3   2

Library of Congress Cataloging-in-Publication Data

Rall, Ted.
    Generalissimo el Busho : essays and cartoons on the Bush / Ted Rall.
    p.cm.
    ISBN 1-56163-384 --ISBN 1-56163-385-2 (pbk.)
    1. United States--Politics and government--2001- 2. United States--Politics and
government--2001---Caricatures and cartoons. 3. Bush, George W. (George Walker),
1946- 4. Bush, George W. (George Walker), 1946---Caricatures and cartoons. 5.
American wit and humor, Pictorial. I. Title.

E902.R35 2004
973.931'092--dc22

                                                                    2004040206

GENERALISSIMO el BUSHO

ESSAYS & CARTOONS ON THE BUSH YEARS

TED RALL

NANTIER · BEALL · MINOUSTCHINE
Publishing inc.
new york

Also Available by Ted Rall from NBM:
My War With Brian, $8.95
2024, $16.95 hc., $9.95 pb.
To Afghanistan and Back, $15.95 hc., $9.95 pb.

Edited by Ted Rall from NBM:
Attitude: The New Subversive Political Cartoonists, $13.95
Attitude 2: The New Subversive Alternative Cartoonists, $13.95

We have over 200 titles, write
for our color catalog:
NBM
555 8th Ave., suite 1202,
New York, NY 10018
www.nbmpublishing.com

Other Books by Ted Rall:
Waking Up in America
All The Rules Have Changed
Revenge of the Latchkey Kids
Search and Destroy
Gas War
Wake Up, You're Liberal!

Ted Rall Online: www.RALL.com

Editor: J.P. Trostle

Front and Back Cover Design: Henry H. Owings

Acknowledgements: David Stanford, Karen Pershing and Maura McLaughlin edited
and proofread the essays, Sue Roush edited the cartoons and Terry Nantier published it.
Anthony Kennedy, Sandra Day O'Connor, William Rehnquist, Antonin Scalia and
Clarence Thomas appointed the subject of this work, Mohammed Atta and eighteen
associates provided him with the opportunity to consolidate power, and the leaders of
the Democratic Party sat on its hands while he made one hell of a mess.

CONTENTS

PART III: WAR WITHOUT JUSTIFICATION, WAR WITHOUT END

PART IV: YEAR OF THE LONG KNIVES

Introduction
by Tom Tomorrow

Somebody really needs to lock Ted Rall up. Not for his own good, or society's—but for mine.

I mean, look at this guy. He writes and draws thirty-eight columns and fifty-seven cartoons a week, and puts out a new book every month and a half. (Okay, I might be slightly off on those numbers, but I don't think by much.) My guess is, he's made a deal with the devil. I believe he has the ability to freeze time itself, enabling him to kick out a week's worth of work while normal cartoonists sit frozen in their bathrobes with their coffee halfway to their lips, staring at a blank sheet of 2-ply bristol. (Little known fact: all cartoonists work in their bathrobes, which are generally encrusted with filth.)

And not only is he preternaturally productive—he's good at what he does. Don't you just hate that?

Ted and I have been competitors for the same small slice of the pie for a long time. Don't get me wrong, I think our work is worlds apart. My cartoon is the one with the penguin, his is the one where people always get shot in the final panel. Could we be more dissimilar? I think not. But we do share a few superficial attributes—we're both excessively verbose, left-leaning cartoonists with a certain, shall we say, *non-traditional* approach to the visual aspect of our craft. So we get pigeonholed together, and when an editor is in the market for a wordy, badly drawn left-wing cartoon, he or she generally chooses one of us over the other—leaving the unlucky one to raise his fist and look upward toward a receding camera and shout, with fury:

"KHAAAAN!"

At least, that's what happens in my house.

The point is, Ted and I have a complicated relationship, which is perhaps summed up best by the following amusing, yet entirely true, anecdote: one evening, many years ago, I stumbled home far too late after spending an evening drinking far too much beer with Ted, arguing about pretty much everything, which is what political cartoonists do for fun when they're not sitting alone in their filth-encrusted bathrobes, contemplating the sheer incomprehensible stupidity of the rest of the world—er, I mean to say, *poking gentle fun at the foibles that make us all human.* At any rate, I climbed into bed, in that way you do when you're fifteen sheets to the wind and you think you're being really, really quiet but in fact you're making more noise than Bill O'Reilly shouting down some hapless liberal college professor, and my wife woke up and rolled over sleepily, and said, "Where have you been–dumping Ted Rall's body in the river?"

Such a kidder, that wife of mine.

I believe Ted once described me in some interview as the bad penny who kept turning up everywhere he wanted to be—which makes absolutely no sense, because *he's* the one who

gets all the gigs *I* want, but there it is.

You get the idea.

However: at a certain point you realize that the only other guy who's doing anything close to what you do is also the only other guy who has even the slightest idea what you go through, and then the story unfolds like your basic buddy movie, in which one cop goes strictly by the book while the other plays by his own rules, and by the end of the movie they have each developed a grudging respect for the other's methods. So now, we chuckle about it all. Like the time I stayed out too late, disposing of his body—it turned out he wasn't really dead at all! Somehow he managed to get loose from the chains and weights and swim to shore! The joke was sure on me there!

I jest, of course, because we are cartoonists, and are expected to be zany and amusing at all times. Even when the subjects with which we deal are crushingly depressing, or horrifying, or maddening, or, most often these past few years, some combination of all these things.

Suffice it to say, I've got some sense of what Ted went through to produce the work compiled in these pages. People often come up to us (and by "us" I mean "me," but I suspect Ted gets this too) and say, "Ha ha, you've sure got a lot of material these days!" and we (and by "we" I mean—oh you know) smile a strained smile and say, "Ha ha, that's certainly true"—but I'll tell you a secret: surprisingly enough, it's not all wackiness and fun, immersing yourself 24/7 in the cesspool of American politics. I mean, sure, mostly wackiness and fun. But sometimes, not.

And since 9/11—well, I don't know if you've noticed, but the country's been kind of divided these past few years. Lot of vitriol being tossed around. Lot of anger, most of it aimed at other Americans.

Actually, at first the country pretended to be united, standing behind a strong and capable leader, and it was a pretty lonely place to be, out there in the cold pointing out that the president was still sort of, you know, a moron—but Rall was out there, you'd better believe it, with a big-ass megaphone, volume turned up high, shouting, "EXCUSE ME, YOU FUCKING IDIOTS, BUT THE PRESIDENT IS *STILL* AN UNELECTED FRAUD!!"

As I write these words, in the winter of 2004, there is a new campaign season upon us and the Democrats seem to have finally developed some vestige of a spine, and suddenly it's okay again for late night comedians and mainstream editorial cartoonists to criticize the president, to suggest, if you will forgive the overused metaphor, that he is standing buck naked in front of all of us, wagging his shrimp-sized dick around as he brags about the jewel-encrusted jock strap in which he claims it is encased. (You know: *that* overused metaphor.)

But here's the thing: saying this stuff when everyone else is saying it is easy. Saying it when the entire country seems to be lined up against you—well, that's when it matters. And even his most severe detractors have to acknowledge, at least in those uncertain moments when a ray of self-doubt momentarily pierces the fog of their self-righteous sloganeering, that Ted Rall has the courage of his convictions.

What I'm trying to say is, when he's trapped in a cabin in the woods surrounded by murderous zombies, Ted's not gonna hesitate to grab that chainsaw and get all Bruce Campbell on your ass.

And speaking of those detractors: oh, my goodness. As he notes in one of the essays compiled herein, the *Wall Street Journal* calls him "the most bitterly anti-American commentator in America." *The National Review* says that he's "a big fat zero, an ignorant, talentless hack with a flair for recycling leftist pieties into snarky cartoons that inspired breakfast-table chuckles among the leftist literati and the granola-munching types."

(Not only does he get all the good gigs, he gets all the good enemies.)

So, this terrible America-hating cartoonist—in what ways, exactly, does he hate America? Well, he hates America so much, he thinks the guy who wins the election should be the guy who actually becomes president. He hates America so much, he thinks an administration that turns a huge surplus into a record deficit should be berated mercilessly for its sheer evil incompetence. Why, he hates America so much, he seems to be pissed off that forty-odd million Americans have no health coverage, and millions of others are either barely scraping by or sleeping out on the street, while the muckety-mucks at Halliburton spend their spare hours diving into swimming pools full of cash like taxpayer-funded Scrooge McDucks.

Ted Rall hates America so much, he wants it to live up to its own ideals.

And don't get me started on how much he doesn't support the troops. Why, he doesn't support them so much, he thinks they should be at home with their families, rather than dying overseas in an unjustified, illegal war.

You can see why the *Wall Street Journal* denounces him with such vigor and passion.

So—to begin nudging this unwieldy monster of an introduction toward something approximating a graceful exit—let me just say that if you're standing in the bookstore trying to decide between this book and the latest compilation of office-related witticisms from Dilbert, well, you should buy this one, because Ted really needs the money, to support his sixteen (at last count) illegitimate children and, of course, to pay off his massive gambling

debts. (If, however, you're standing there trying to decide between this one and one of mine, you'll just have to let your conscience guide you to the best decision, which is, obviously, to buy both.)

I won't kid you. These drawings, and these words—you'll laugh, but they'll make you angry. Mostly at Generalissimo El Busho, and his ragged band of crazed right-wing revolutionaries—but probably at Ted, too. (The cartoon where he advocates drowning helpless kittens and putting adorable babies in concentration camps—it might seem a bit over the top to you. But hey, that's Ted.)

In all seriousness, that's his job, to piss you off and make you think. It sounds banal, but there it is. It's his job, and he's good at it.

Tom Tomorrow
February 2004

Preface
by Ted Rall

Artists and writers serve as effective critics only when they enjoy some special insight into their targets. Long-time *Washington Post* cartoonist Herblock understood Richard Nixon's underlying personality and depicted his sleazy essence with a dozen scowling lines surrounding a grim lattice of five o'clock shadow. The *Seattle Times'* David Horsey channeled to the core of Bill Clinton's sexual dualism, his simultaneous admiration for and exploitation of women, using fulsome young lasses pursued by the Arkansan Apollo. Horsey got Clinton to an extent that other editorial artists, me included, were unable to do. I've cartooned every American president since Ronald Reagan and I think I've done some decent pieces about them, but I didn't possess unique insight into their personalities.

Bush is different. Maybe it's because I've had experience with bullies. I know one when I see one and Bush is a bully.

Before the 2000 election crisis that spiraled around the contested state of Florida, it wasn't obvious that Bush was a thug. If Al Gore had campaigned for a third term of Clinton's economy minus Bill's sexcapades, George W. Bush had presented himself as a third generation photocopy of his father. Compassionate conservatism echoed a thousand points of light; his repeated pledge not to engage in nation building an indicator of an introverted foreign policy that wouldn't have airlifted a tank to invade Panama, much less Iraq. My primary objections to a Dubya presidency concerned its dynastic pretensions—Adamses and Roosevelts aside, a nation with fewer than fifty presidents to its name ought to be able to find its leaders in new families each and every time—and the man's lack of intellectual qualifications. Simply put, Bush was too simple to be president.

America awoke the morning after November 7, 2000 to find Florida, and by extension the presidency, tied in a statistical dead heat. When the Florida recount began, Gore assumed two personas. His "let's wait and see" public demeanor belied his hiring of legal experts to study what could be done behind the scenes to push the state's crucial twenty-five electoral votes into his column. It was, in other words, politics as usual.

Bush, on the other hand, tried to project an air of inevitability about the outcome. Two days later, more than a month before the United States Supreme Court ruled on Bush v. Gore, the Bush campaign sent former Secretary of State James Baker to PBS' *The News Hour with Jim Lehrer* to make its position known. "The vote here in Florida was very close, but when it was counted, Governor Bush was the winner," said Baker. Incredibly, as the

recount continued, Baker returned to Lehrer's show to threaten a military coup d'état should Bush be denied the presidency.

Bush's people hired young goons to beat up and intimidate Miami-Dade County election workers. They asked Republican members of the military to mail in their absentee ballots after they'd missed the Election Day deadline. They opened a Bush-Cheney transition office, even going so far as to announce their cabinet picks—all while the state of Florida was continuing to count ballots.

Bush was a bully. Like all bullies—like all tin-pot Third World autocrats—he wasn't going to take no for an answer.

The first man in American history to illegally seize power was appointed president by a party-line vote of the Supreme Court on December 20, 2000. The first image that popped into my mind upon watching Bush's simian countenance "accept" Gore's concession was that of former dictator Augusto Pinochet. I discovered an old *Time* containing a state portrait of the Chilean general; I was struck first by the contrast between the grandeur of his costume and the dimness of his eyes.

The parallel with Bush was readily apparent. Like Pinochet, he would soon assume all of the trappings of high office—Air Force One, honor guards, the right to interrupt prime-time TV sit-coms—but they wouldn't change his essential inferiority and incompetence. Bush was the consummate bullshit artist. He'd bullshitted his way into Yale with a sub-par 1206 SAT, bullshitted his way into personal wealth by scamming taxpayers into financing a corrupt stadium deal, and bullshitted his way into the White House by wielding vague threats of violence while dodging questions about his past as a draft-dodging coke addict.

I vowed to never forget, never to "move on." Were Bush's ersatz presidency to be recognized and accepted, it would create a terrible precedent. Similar transgressions might occur in the future. American democracy might never get back on track. I promised myself that I would never utter the phrase "President George W. Bush," but that wasn't enough. As a cartoonist I needed to create a character that served to constantly remind readers that Bush was not only illegitimate, but also a buffoon. I drew the empty-eyed, bat-eared Bush in General Pinochet's uniform, festooned with medals, a sash and a great big hat. Eureka! Generalissimo El Busho was born.

Cartoonists will tell you that the job often feels like stuffing a drawing into a bottle and tossing it into the ocean in hope that someone somewhere will enjoy it. We rarely get feedback, and when we do, it's almost all negative. Reactions to my early El Busho cartoons varied from stony silence to friendly confusion. If that's Bush, why don't you just draw him wearing a suit?

I tried that for a few weeks after the judicial coup. Then the mail started pouring in. "Where's the Generalissimo?" "Bring back El Busho!" The people "got" him. I brought him back in time for his coronation, er, inauguration.

Of course, Bush truly *became* the Generalissimo after 9/11. He grew into his medals and oversized hat by launching two equally unjustified (and unwinnable) wars in as many years, assassinating innocent American citizens, opening a concentration camp and dozens of secret internment facilities for those he declared "enemy combatants." The fascist bully who'd stolen the presidency revealed himself as the warmongering fascist of the passed-without-debate USA PATRIOT Act and of imaginary Iraqi weapons of mass destruction. Too many of my fellow pundits and cartoonists, stunned by the horrors of New York and Washington and Pennsylvania, and its subsequent knee-jerk nationalism, began pulling their punches after 9/11. Not me. If Bush hadn't changed, why should I?

Now that the national media, emboldened by an election and the passage of time, is asking Bush tough questions about Iraq (and even Afghanistan), it's easy to forget how lonely it was for those of us—pundits, journalists, citizens—who dared to speak up about the threat Bush posed (and poses) to our great nation in the year or two after 9/11. I received countless death threats; my favorite came from the New York police officer who helpfully left his name and rank on my voicemail along with a promise to slit not only my throat, but my wife's (his precinct number appeared on my caller ID). Who was I going to call, the cops?

Occasionally, a creative person conceives something that's bigger than he or she. "Generalissimo El Busho" the character—the phrase—has caught on. Perhaps because I was one of the first commentators to understand what Bush and his gang of neofascist bullies are all about, because I was one of the first to dare to say it relentlessly, it works. I wish it didn't, but it does.

Ted Rall
March 2004

THE SEIZURE OF POWER

The Trivializing of American Politics

"They are now spending more money on advertising than they are on innovation. Join with me, and we will stand up to the big drug companies, and we will guarantee prescription drugs as a matter of right for every senior in America."

—Al Gore, July 6, 2000

OCTOBER 10, 2000—The recent history of the United States is a litany of lost opportunities. Never has that been clearer than during this sad, pathetic, duller than death election year. "These debates are good things," George W. Bush told listeners at the Marion, Illinois airport on October 7. "I like the debates because it became pretty clear to people that we've got huge differences [with the Democratic ticket]," he said.

Of course, the truth is the polar opposite. What's become painfully clear in recent weeks is how similar Gore and Bush, as well as their parties, really are. Both men favor free trade, both are pro-choice (though Bush prefers to shut up about it) and both are exactly as exhilarating as a first-period freshman microeconomics lecture. Even more striking, however, is how stylistically identical they are: both the second-rate son of the obscure defeated New Deal senator and the second-rate son of the inarticulate defeated president consistently ignore America's massive, pressing structural issues in favor of trivial micro-mini issuettes calibrated to bring in a hundred votes here, a thousand votes there.

There are big issues. It's just that no one's talking about them. All over America, parents worry that their children are receiving a substandard public education. Many of them are right to worry. Books are out of date, schools are falling apart and teacher salaries are too low to attract reasonably qualified professionals, much less the best and the brightest our kids deserve. Beyond high school, many parents—even those in the upper end of the middle class—face an awful choice between taking out second mortgages and saddling their kids with huge student loans to pay for college.

These are huge, systemic problems. Public schools remain in chronic crisis because they're funded and regulated locally, which necessarily means that students' education varies in quality, depending on which town they happen to reside. College tuition is unaffordable because the United States is one of the few industrialized nations that doesn't have a predominantly public post-secondary school system. Systemic problems require systemic solu-

tions. Replacing local control of schools with a European-style federal system would be an obvious remedy. Another would be making college free to those qualified to attend. With the economy cooking along nicely, we're never going to have a better chance to address these long neglected issues—but no one's on the job.

So what do Mssrs. Bush and Gore propose? Gore's ideas include universal preschool, smaller class sizes and a $10,000 tax credit for college tuition. Bush wants $1,500 school vouchers that public school kids could use for private school tuition and, um, even more of the local control of public schools that's at the root of our problems. Smart or dumb, it's all penny ante stuff; no one has ever passed up private school because they were $1,500 short of the average $8,000-per-year tuition. No one has ever lost out on a college education because they were $10,000 short of a $100,000 tuition bill. Americans need education subsidies, not coupons.

Similarly, Generation Xers—who pay more into Social Security than any other generation before them—are currently projected to get exactly zero out of the system by the time they retire at age 69 (the retirement age has been quietly jacked up, effective 2028). Gore, courting the Baby Boomer vote, doesn't see a problem with sticking it to his own daughters. Bush proposes partial privatization of the system, a ridiculous scheme that would mess things up even worse during a recession and isn't sufficiently comprehensive to save the day even if the current boom continues forever—which isn't going to happen.

Even on the relatively minor issue of high gas prices, the two candidates managed to wallow in inconsequential drivel throughout the campaign. Bush's solution: Allow oil companies to drill in Alaska's Arctic National Wildlife Refuge (ANWR) and demand that other

oil-producing nations guarantee us a steady oil supply (as if previous presidents didn't do that anyway). Gore, meanwhile, would offer "up to" (i.e., less than) $6,000 to families who buy fuel efficient cars. He would also double the tax credit for wind-powered generators.

Weird.

I've got news for both of these guys: Neither crapping up the Great White North nor bribing motorists into buying Geo Metros is going to get us dollar-a-gallon gas next week, next year or next decade. What would? Financing Kazakhstan's proposed Caspian Sea-to-Mediterranean pipeline project in exchange for a big share of that country's huge new oil strike, or banning SUVs, for starters—but neither candidate has either the imagination or the guts to back this level of meaningful change.

Perhaps the ultimate example of the two candidates' unwillingness to confront America's big problems is their teensy-weensy approach to health care. Gore wants to cover prescription drug costs under Medicare, but only for senior citizens—and then only for low-income senior citizens. Bush's problem with that? The Gore plan requires enrollees to sign up at age 64 1/2 or be locked out of the system forever. Forty-four million Americans remain completely uninsured. Millions more have their requests for reimbursements routinely rejected by the big HMOs. You wouldn't know it to hear what passes for the debate, but prescription drugs are actually the cheapest of medical costs. Countless patients die because they can't afford operations. Americans need and want socialized medicine, and they need it yesterday—not the watered-down Hillary plan of 1993, but the real deal, where doctors become federal employees. Instead Bush and Gore are worried about covering prescription drugs for the wealthiest age group in the country.

What's next: tax credits for Band-Aids?

George W. Bush: The Churamanian Dandicate?

Republican presidential nominee George W. Bush on Tuesday denied suggestions in a Vanity Fair article that he has dyslexia. "No, I'm not dyslexic," Bush said on ABC's Good Morning America. "That's all I can tell you." The article in the magazine's October issue quotes language experts who say Bush's tendency to mix up words while speaking is consistent with dyslexia, a neurological disorder impairing the ability to read and write. Bush's presidential campaign, said the author, Gail Sheehy, may have confused the Texas governor with his brother, Neil, who has dyslexia."

—*Associated Press, September 12, 2000*

SEPTEMBER 12, 2000—Now is the time for all good inarticulate men to come to the aid of George W. Bush. As the issue of their candidate's intellectual acuity—brain power unfavorably compared to Dan Quayle's—continues to dog the GOP, Democratic detractors are upping the ante. He's not merely stupid, some Democrats are saying. Now they're asserting that Bush's famously tortured grammar and syntax indicate that the guy suffers from a learning disability and is therefore mentally unqualified to hold high office.

"Based on his speech and behavior, his hyperactivity and impulsivity, you can say there is a possibility of some sort of disorder," Dr. Irwin Rosenthal of the New York Association for the Learning Disabled told the *New York Daily News*. "If he were in a New York City school, they would pick up on this and say, 'Let's check out this person.'" Rosenthal was responding to a widely touted Gail Sheehy spread in *Vanity Fair* magazine about the Texas governor.

Following in the tradition of his dimwitted father (and possibly his dyslexic brother Neil), George W. has ejaculated some spectacular verbal sequences—evidence, expert Nancy LaFevers told Sheehy, that is "consistent with dyslexia." Dyslexia, called "word blindness" during less enlightened times, causes those who suffer from it to have trouble reading, typically because they mentally transpose or confuse letters and digits.

Sheehy cites classic Bushisms like "Reading is the basics for all learning," "Put food on your family" and "The Senator cannot have it both ways. He can't take the high horse and then claim the low road" as proof that after January 20, 2001 we may have a guy sitting in the Oval Office without the mental faculties to remember the launch codes or, if he does, to

input them in correct sequence—which, when you think about it, might not be such a bad thing. Sue Horn, former president of the Maryland branch of the International Dyslexia Association, adds helpfully: "Bush is probably dyslexic, although he has probably never been diagnosed."

"No the governor does not have dyslexia," Bush Communications Director Karen Hughes retorted. He said, she said, but in what order?

Sheehy also argues that Bush has ADD—attention deficit disorder—because he avoids long meetings and reserves three and a half hours each day to work out and play video games. Since Bush isn't all that buff, I'm willing to bet that at least two of those hours involve working up to level four on "Doom."

Kidding aside, these are serious allegations. We can't have the commander-in-chief of the armed forces of a relatively important nation declaring war when he really meant to proposition an intern. What if Bush were to dial the wrong number on the red phone and accidentally make friends with Fidel? Today's free trade agreements are incredibly complex. What if Bush spaced out and forgot to sell out American workers to transnational corporate interests?

I'm no fan, but I think Bush is getting a bit of a bum rap. As a former talk radio host, I've listened to hundreds of hours of my own yapping on tape. Though most of my friends would probably tell you that I've mastered the English language, a reporter looking for evidence of dyslexia or ADD in my recorded programs would find it in spades. Malapropisms, faulty tense conjugations, mixing up singles and plurals, not being able to summon just the right word to describe a thought—signs of mental flubberosity are all there on magnetic tape. Even the most eloquent television personalities, people who rely on their command of

speech to earn their livings, manage to blow a sentence or a phrase every now and then. If every candidate is held responsible for such oratorical screw-ups, no one can withstand the level of scrutiny that goes with running for office.

When a public speaker blows a word or a line, moreover, he faces an immediate dilemma: If he corrects himself, he breaks the flow of his speech and risks braking momentum. If he doesn't, listeners may assume he's learning-disabled. On the air, I usually opted to just keep going; that's probably what Bush does too.

As for the ADD thing, how many of us actually enjoy long meetings? To be sure, love of brevity can go too far, such as when Ronald Reagan limited all memos crossing his desk to a single page. But I'm with Bush when it comes to such confabs. America would be a far better place if meetings were kept short, sweet, or better yet, nonexistent.

That leaves us with the video game issue. The first item to emphasize is that we don't know whether Bush favors the medium's most popular genre: violent shoot-'em-ups. Experts like Robert Grossman, who wrote a comprehensive study of what makes soldiers willing to shoot strangers on demand called *On Killing*, have long claimed that the digitized death depicted in such games desensitizes their players to real violence. The United States military agrees; it uses them to train troops to aim to kill. So, while Bush may or may not be dyslexic, the discussion should nonetheless elicit concern. The revelation that he's addicted to video games may explain his practice of signing death warrants more frequently than other people write checks. Perhaps he no longer views the hundred-plus inmates he's dispatched to be poisoned to death as real people. Maybe he views each one as one more point toward some diabolical judicial endgame, one in which crime is gone because all the criminals are dead.

Or maybe he's just a mean dumbass. If things go wrong, we'll find out in January.

One Scam, One Vote

It's understandable that Bush wants to shut the process down while he's ahead, although it's risky to be perceived as having won the presidency after ballots were thrown out in a state run by your brother. But what is everybody else's hurry? It will be hard enough for anyone to govern without a rush to judgment setting off a cottage industry of the grassy-knoll variety. Do we want "Who Stole Florida?" on the shelf alongside "Who Shot JFK?"
—Margaret Carlson, Time, November 13, 2000

NOVEMBER 14, 2000—It's not a crisis, at least not a constitutional one. Back in 1787, the Founders of Our Glorious Republic weren't troubled by the possibility that it might take days, weeks and maybe even months to find out who'd been elected president. But the closest election ever—let's face it, it'll never come down to two or three hundred votes in a national race again—has proven that the world's supposed best political system sucks just as badly as those in countries that don't bother trying to behave like a superpower. And that has far graver consequences than a mere crisis. This is possibly the beginning of the end of American democracy, which is, admittedly, just another way of saying "crisis." We may survive this thing intact; then again, maybe not.

Whatever—why should I be any less confused than any other American this week?

We don't know who will ultimately end up with Alan Greenspan's home number, whether it'll be a legislative or a judicial process or even whether a resolution will occur quickly enough to prevent Dennis Hastert from assuming office as *de facto* prez on January 20. Nobody knows what comes next, but it isn't too early to draw some disturbing conclusions:

This Election is Totally Screwed, Period. If George W. Bush takes office on the strength of Florida's deeply flawed voting process, he will forever be regarded as an illegitimate president. Bush's ascension was queered by more factors than the West Palm Beach "butterfly" ballots, his lawsuit to prevent a manual recount and the sudden discovery of thousands of missing votes within days of November 7. The same folks who believe in UFOs and the man on the grassy knoll—which is to say nearly everyone—will never be convinced that Jeb didn't dip his fraternal paws into the state Board of Elections. True or not, the perception of conflict of interest became the reality of conspiracy. Bush's henchmen, after all, phoned the networks within minutes of their premature Gore-gets-Florida call to tell them they'd messed up.

Why were the Bushies so positive so soon that they'd snagged Florida?

23

Other states, like New Mexico, with its four vote differential, ended up even more evenly divided than Florida. But the GOP didn't challenge the flawed calls in those places. Why not? Down on the street, there's little talk about injunctions and absentee ballots. Everyone's gossiping about the Jeb Factor.

This weird situation isn't likely to turn out any better for Al Gore. At this point, his only road to the White House winds through a maze of messy legal challenges. Americans hate lawyers, plaintiffs, all that stuff. Should he ultimately prevail over Bush, Gore will be our first judicially selected president. Even liberal Democrats, relieved that the school-prayer-anti-abortion-creationist barbarians have been kept at bay another four years, will have a tough time respecting a president who ascended to high office due to some obscure election law interpreted by a judge they've never heard of.

No matter what happens, neither Gore nor Bush will receive, nor will they deserve, any props whatsoever. They were both punks during the race, they're acting like punks now—and punks they shall remain.

The United States is a Third World Country. Any high-tech nation that can drop a bomb straight down Saddam's chimney, time the outcome of the Indianapolis 500 down to hundredths of a second and measure the net worth of Microsoft Corp. by the second to the penny ought to be able to handle integers. Well, you'd think so anyway. Despite recent barks to the contrary, one vote really doesn't make a difference. Normally, even tens of thousands of votes don't have a determinant effect on elections; it took this year's statistical anomaly to bring our incredibly sloppy system to light.

Consider Florida's first automatic recount. Bush saw his lead over Gore trimmed by about 1,300 votes, but between the two of them, the Board of Elections somehow found more than 2,000 votes that they had missed the first time—using the same workers, the same machines and the same counting methods as before. Multiply that same statistical variance by fifty states, and you've got 100,000 votes—potentially enough to cost Gore's 200,000-vote lead over Bush in the national popular vote. Add in confusing ballots, failed systems (punch cards that don't punch all the way through) and good old-fashioned corruption (hi, Jeb!), and you have a system unworthy of running a church bingo parlor, much less electing the President of the United States.

The Rest of the World Is On To Us. During election week alone, the U.S. State Department criticized election results in Tanzania, Egypt, Azerbaijan and Kyrgyzstan, asserting that balloting in those countries had been marred by fraud and harassment. How on earth can we expect our campaign to spread democracy throughout the world to suceed when we don't have a viable one ourselves? That sound you hear drifting across the big water is foreigners laughing at our hypocritical clueless asses.

In a Way, We're Lucky. Thanks to the bizarro Gore-Bush non-presidency, we now have the opportunity to fix long-neglected problems with our voting system. If we're smart, we'll adopt a federalized system of balloting so that future problems, if any, will be uniform and thus easier to repair. We can work to relieve overcrowded precincts, outlaw harassment of minority voters and develop forms that any idiot, even those senile old goats in West Palm Beach County, can figure out. But more than anything else, officials should go over the 2000 election results with a fine-toothed comb. Wherever there's the slightest doubt about confusing ballots, discarded votes and other issues, they should be thoughtfully addressed. And if it takes a few dozen judges to make sure that every single vote was counted in the manner in which it was cast, so be it.

The Jeb Factor

In the days leading up to the presidential election, Florida Governor Jeb Bush promised his brother, Republican nominee George W. Bush, that he would nail down Florida's 25 electoral votes—a promise on which he could still deliver. The Florida Legislature is poised to hold a special session to consider naming a slate of electors on their own. With a strong Republican majority in both houses, those electors are likely to be pledged to George W. Bush. Under Florida law, if a bill sits on the governor's desk for seven days, it automatically becomes law. But with lawmakers' go-ahead with a special session, Jeb Bush has made it clear he would consider signing a bill naming electors. "Depends on what the bill is that would be presented to me. I can't pass judgment on legislation until I see it," Bush said Thursday. "But if the question is, if the bill is acceptable, would I sign it rather than allow it to become law without my signature—yeah, I'd sign it."
—*CNN, December 1, 2000*

DECEMBER 5, 2000—There's plenty of room for reasonable disagreement in this post-election netherworld. The Bushies are right that we need a president-elect and that we needed him weeks ago. Despite lackadaisical opinion polls and a surprisingly high level of public apathy, the legal maneuvering over recounts can't go on forever. Yet Gore's peeps have a point too, a far more pressing one. As everybody now knows, our votes don't all count—not by a long shot—and while it doesn't matter in most elections, there's probably no better time to remedy that situation than a disputed contest with a five hundred-something vote spread. The tension between the need for speed and the desire for accuracy has people of all political stripes spewing contradictions, lies and faulty syllogisms, but it's not because they're ill-intentioned: They're just angry that their guy came so damned close.

Then, far beyond the ideological confines where most of us dwell, is the unparalleled cynicism of Florida Governor Jeb Bush.

Democrats talk darkly about confusing ballots and cops patting down blacks en route to the polls. Republicans call the flurry of litigation clogging Florida courts—which they started, by the way, but never mind—nothing short of a attempted judicial coup d'état. But no member of either party has sunk as low as Jeb, who (get this) actually says that he'll sign a law to make his brother president.

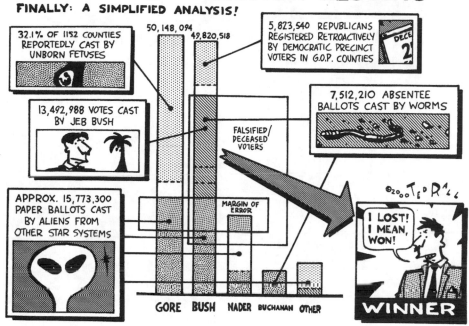

No one blames the public for suffering from post-election fatigue. During the past few weeks, the *New York Times* has run a separate "Counting the Vote" section every day. The paper's crisis section contains such highlights as a county-by-county statistical-regression analysis of the Buchanan vote and a chart indicating which hearings will occur in what court during the coming week, but nothing about the stuff we really care about: Why does Gore's daughter look hot from far away but not from up close? Can a man who names his dog "Spot" be trusted with the keys to the missile silos?

"Counting the Vote" offers little of the drama of the great media feeding frenzies of the recent past. Falling chads have replaced thong underwear. Katherine Harris has filled in for Kathleen Willey. And try as CNN might, the Board of Elections' yellow Ryder truck will never fill the wheel treads of O.J.'s white Bronco. Clinton's history and the good times he wrought are coming to an end. So it isn't surprising that people have moved past the election back to the normal staples of American life: bad TV, bad food and bad parenting.

Still: Jeb Bush says that he would sign a bill that assigns Florida's 25 electoral votes to his brother.

It shouldn't matter which of these guys you'd rather see win. Even if you're a devoted Republican, it should be apparent that a president who takes office thanks to his brother's signature on a piece of paper may not only be doomed as a leader but may take the whole damned republic out the door with him.

Of course Gore can only emerge victorious if he wins some tortured court battles. That sucks for him, and even more for Bush, but in that scenario, at least Gore would prevail after manipulating the system. It'd be barely legit, but it would be legit nonetheless. But if Jeb signs a bill anointing his brother as ersatz president, it will violate the basic ethical and legal

premise of conflict of interest and reduce the United States to a global pariah. It's unbelievable that an American citizen would consider debasing himself by committing such a vile act, that he'd talk about it in public, and that George W. hasn't already issued a statement refusing to take office under his brother's signature.

There remain, of course, several honorable options for the Bush camp. They can fight it out in the courts and hope that they win the key cases before the December 12 deadline for selecting Florida's electors. Even if they miss the deadline—which is more of a suggestion than a legal requirement—and Gore wins the Electoral College vote, there's no constitutional prohibition against continuing to litigate. If Bush keeps his Florida popular vote lead after all the votes are ultimately counted, no one will question his legitimacy—even if it takes until next December to do so.

Alternatively, Florida can forfeit its electoral votes, making Al Gore the next president, 267 to 245. Bush would lose, but he'd lose legally (even though it's too late for either man to lose gracefully). But, for a patriot, losing a presidential race is a tiny indignity compared to the political abomination currently being contemplated by The Brother. If Jeb signs that bill, he will be committing the greatest crime against democracy in American history.

The Resistance Begins Now

Soon to be the 43rd president of the United States, Republican George W. Bush turned Wednesday to the twin challenges of constructing a government and uniting a nation divided. Al Gore scripted his exit from a tortuously close campaign that will live in history. Victorious Republicans, in conciliatory and sympathetic tones, prepared to claim control of both the White House and Congress for the first time in more than 45 years, while Democrats talked ominously of deep partisan schisms to condemn the U.S. Supreme Court ruling that pushed Gore from the race. Bush has said he hopes to "seize the moment" if the courts ruled in his favor. "Part of seizing the moment is reaching out to the other party, to show his bipartisanship," said Bush spokesman Ari Fleischer.
—Associated Press, December 13, 2000

DECEMBER 19, 2000—George W. Bush is not the president-elect of the United States of America. George W. Bush has no more right to move into 1600 Pennsylvania Avenue than I have. Every law that George W. Bush signs during the next four years will be exactly as meaningless as a blank sheet of paper, because he will not be legally authorized to hold that office. His appointees deserve neither power nor respect, since they will be exercising functions for an impostor president. Call him Governor Bush—once a governor, always a governor. Call him the Resident, the Thief-in-Chief, whatever. Just don't call him president.

Al Gore's concession speech does not make George W. Bush president-elect; that the media (and maybe even Gore himself) got tired of fighting Bush's lawyers in the courts doesn't make any difference. The presidency is not a chess match to be forfeited by the exhausted to the energetic.

An ABC News *Washington Post* poll reveals that 42 percent of Americans do not accept George W. Bush as the legitimately elected leader of the free world, and they are correct. If the election were held today, Gore would win by 17 to 42 percent—a landslide that speaks more to quiet disgust with Generalissimo El Busho's sleazy commandeering of the White House than any affection for the outgoing vice president.

We waited patiently as a bewildering array of lawsuits wound their way through Florida and federal courts. When it came to light that in a typical election two percent of votes are not counted nationally—two percent!—Americans were naturally shocked, but we assumed that the long-standing ballot-counting problem would finally be corrected, after it had

caused an all but unresolvable tie in a presidential election. When El Busho's brother Jeb threatened to sign a bill assigning Florida's twenty-five electoral votes to the GOP, we trusted that he'd never get the chance rather than react precipitously.

We may never know who really won Florida. Even a consistent statewide counting standard would have been subjective, as will be any study done by reporters or professors after the fact. Florida's punchcard system was designed for disaster; the best it could do is yield approximate election returns.

The Supreme Court's right-wingers not only ruled in favor of the right-wing candidate, they cynically ran out the clock (a non-existent clock at that) to justify their ruling. First they suspended Florida's statewide recount on Saturday, December 9, three days before Florida was scheduled to pick its electors on the 12th. (Actually, the electors could have been picked as late as the 18th; afterwards, an Electoral College vote could still have been overturned by the Supreme Court. Even the January 20 inaugural isn't truly a deadline; under the Constitution, Speaker of the House Dennis Hastert would become Acting President until the matter was ultimately resolved.)

First and foremost, election disputes fall under the jurisdiction of state courts. Federal courts, of which the U.S. Supreme Court is the highest body, cannot hear lawsuits related to election disputes. Beyond this crucial constitutional distinction were garden-variety dirty tricks. While the Supremes issued their stay on a Saturday, they refused to hear the case until Monday. (The Court, it seems, only works weekends for the Republicans. Democrats must await regular office hours.) They issued their decision at 10 p.m. on Tuesday the 12th: Ordinarily, the justices ruled, we would have sent this matter back to the Florida Supreme Court with an order to create uniform, statewide ballot-counting standards to resolve the equal protection problem, but now it's too late—because we made it too late, natch.

If you read between the lines of the opinion, you could almost see their toothy grins.

If there's really an equal protection issue in Florida because of vote counting disparities, then *every* election in the country is unconstitutional. More importantly, the Court purposefully dragged out the case to the December 12 deadline to make sure that the Florida vote would never be counted.

Al Gore ought to have spoken the plain truth when he conceded: Neither Bush nor Gore had been elected president—at least not until Florida recounted its votes in accordance with the instructions of its state Supreme Court. That is, after all, the election system we have in this country.

There's a fifty-fifty chance that George W. Bush would have won a statewide recount. If he had, he would now be the legitimate, though barely elected, President of the United States. But Bush and Bush's Supreme Court didn't want to take that chance. Bush was willing to become an illegitimate, illegally installed pretender instead. Now that he has made that decision and benefited therefrom, there's no reason that we shouldn't call him exactly what he is.

The vast majority of Americans, even Gore partisans, hasn't noticed that our representative democracy was suspended on December 12. History, however, is never made by a majority. If it had been up to the majority, there wouldn't be a United States. We'd still be a British colony. Destiny is determined by the few people who know what's right, fight for it against all odds, and set an example for the rest of us to follow. And if you are one of those people, you know one simple fact:

George W. Bush is NOT the president-elect of the United States of America.

Uncle Tom's Cabinet

Retired General Colin Powell, a son of the South Bronx who rose to become America's highest ranking military officer, accepted President-elect Bush's nomination as secretary of state Saturday, pledging to strengthen U.S. alliances and stand firm against nations that practice terrorism. "We will defend our interests from a position of strength," Powell said. With tears in his eyes, Bush praised his first Cabinet pick as "an American hero, an American example and a great American story." If Powell is confirmed, as is expected, he will become the first black secretary of state—just as he was the first black to serve as chairman of the Joint Chiefs of Staff. The appointment is the first for Bush's national security team and his Cabinet. On Sunday, he will name Stanford University administrator Condoleezza Rice, who is also black, as his national security adviser.

—Associated Press, December 16, 2000

DECEMBER 26, 2000—In a brazen attempt to soothe an uncannily apathetic former electorate's concerns about his recent coup d'état, Generalissimo El Busho has done more to create an administration "that looks like America" than Bill Clinton. At first glance, anyway.

The appointment of General Colin Powell as secretary of state, one of the nation's leading black Republicans—or more precisely, one of its only black Republicans—came as little surprise to Washington Kremlinologists. Though coy about his party affiliation back in 1992 when he briefly considered an independent run for the presidency, Powell quickly made a name for himself as one of the military's most outspoken opponents of Clinton's watered-down "don't ask, don't tell" policy concerning gay servicemen and women. He'd been a conservative all along.

Powell's appointment put minority advocacy organizations in a terrible pinch.

On the one hand, the Republican Party's base is stridently, if quietly, racist. The GOP opposed the Voting Rights Act, the Civil Rights Act and virtually every single piece of legislation designed to make life for American blacks a tad less unpleasant. It's an organization that tolerates former Klansman David Duke not just as a member, but as a full-fledged state party official, and its quadrennial conventions feature an ocean of faces whiter than an aisle full of Wonder Bread.

On the other hand, a black man (not the descendant of slaves to be sure, but of Jamaican

immigrants and therefore possessing the requisite skin tone) had been appointed to one of the top ten jobs in the country. Who *cares* if he's a right-wing homophobic bigot?

"Congratulations are in order," NAACP President Kweisi Mfume gushed. "I think most Americans will feel good about this choice." The straight ones, anyway.

In the following week, Bush piled on politically correct appointments of right-wing ideologues. "Fiercely pro-business" Texas Supreme Court Justice Alberto Gonzales, a Latino who served as Governor Bush's adviser on executing state inmates and who repeatedly ruled that teenage girls should have to obtain parental consent to obtain abortions, has been named White House Counsel. Dr. Condoleezza Rice, a black woman who served on Bush's dad's National Security Counsel during the late 1980s—where she helped plan the illegal invasion of Panama and the subsequent arrest and framing of that country's president—landed the national security adviser job. Fanatic anti-Castro Cuban refugee Mel Martinez was picked to become secretary of housing and urban development. Bush the First's Deputy Agriculture Secretary Ann Veneman scored the number one Agriculture job and whiter than white New Jersey Governor Christi(n)e Todd Whitman—the "n" comes and goes—will head the Environmental Protection Agency. Wanna work for Bush? Gotta be white or right.

This looks, but hardly feels, like America.

Democrats, who watched haplessly and helplessly as the White House was stolen by an outlaw Supreme Court, have stood by in silent amazement as an El Busho who ran on a platform of inclusive "compassionate conservatism" assembled a cabinet exclusively composed of right-wing conservatives. (And while it's easy to be distracted by Whitman's pro-choice stance, all of these people are conservative where it counts—in the departments they'll be heading.) Only one Bush nomination, that of wacky Christian fundamentalist

Senator John Ashcroft for attorney general, faces a serious Senate confirmation challenge—and he's a white guy. As long as you dress your right-wing business shills up in skirts and PC melanin, Bush has proven, liberals won't squawk.

In the aftermath of Bush's coup, soft-liberal pundits opined—and GOP spokesmen tacitly agreed—that the squeaker election that wasn't would necessitate a bipartisan approach to governance. If things had gone the other way, if Al Gore had assumed the office that he won, Gore would surely have appointed a Republican or two to his cabinet. But Republicans never make concessions to the left, and the Generalissimo is no exception to this ironclad rule. By dragging up every right-wing woman and minority figure he can to serve on his team, Bush has cleverly created the illusion of, in Dr. Rice's words, "an administration that is bipartisan and perhaps most importantly, an administration that affirms that united we stand, divided we fall." These blacks, Hispanics and women share their politics with uptight white males, but a disorganized Left needlessly obsessed with identity politics can't allow themselves to speak the truth, or even their truth:

Progressives are better off being governed by white male liberals than by a bunch of right-wing nuts who "look like America."

Tie Presidential Pay to Performance

The House voted overwhelmingly Thursday to give members of Congress a $4,600 pay raise in January and to double the next president's salary to $400,000. Lawmakers voted 276-147 to increase their own pay, rolling up nearly 2-1 margins among Republicans and Democrats alike.
—Alan Fram, Associated Press, July 16, 1999

In 1999, real median household income increased for the fifth consecutive year, reaching $40,816.
—Population Resource Center

Poverty deepened and household income fell in 2002, according to the latest report by the U.S. Bureau of the Census. These data mark the second consecutive year in which poverty rose and real income fell for middle-class households, suggesting that both the recession and ensuing weak recovery have eroded Americans' living standards.
—Economic Policy Institute

JANUARY 23, 2001—By any objective standard, it's a tad early to decide whether or not George W. Bush is doing a good job. He's still finding his way around the office, meeting his coworkers for the first time and trying to figure out how to forward phone calls from foreign leaders to De Facto President Dick Cheney. But he's already gotten a pay raise nonetheless.

And we're not talking about some pissant four or five percent raise, like you and I get annually if we're good little drones and don't get caught lingering too long by the Coke machine. We're talking one hundred percent here.

Last year the Republican Congress, anticipating that Bush would become America's CEO, quietly passed a presidential pay increase unlike any other in American history. Clinton earned $200,000 each year; Bush will get $400,000 doing the same job.

The biggest economic problem in America is stagnant wages. The average American family of four earns no more in inflation-adjusted dollars now than it did in 1970, yet

between the four of them, they're working twenty-four more weeks a year than they did then. But that money has hardly vanished into the economic ether. CEO and executive pay has skyrocketed along with the stock market, even allowing for last year's slide in tech stocks. You're working a quarter of your day not for yourself, but for some overweight, middle-aged white guy you've never met—a guy who fully expects you to be satisfied with a four or five percent pay raise in a country that just happens to have a four to five percent rate of inflation.

It's a direct transfer of wealth from the working class to the leisure class.

Paying Americans for being more productive is fair, but if socioeconomic justice doesn't move you to do the right thing, consider your stock portfolio. Two-thirds of economic activity is driven by consumer spending. Pay people more and they spend more, which increases sales and makes your stocks more valuable. The boom economy of the 1990s wasn't just about dot-coms. The big story of the economy, what created a boom that was felt by the average worker, was that it created labor shortages. Workers were scarce. That gave them negotiating power as well as spending power. Now that mass layoffs are starting again, look for anemic spending and a possible slide into recession.

This is all basic stuff, but Bush II gets it no more than his dad did. There is, however, a creative, fair way to tie the president's fate to the people's: Cut the president's pay back to $200,000 and tie his wages to those of the average salaried worker. If the average full-time American employee receives a five percent raise this year, then raise Bush's pay to $210,000. But if the same worker's workweek increases ten percent—effectively cutting his net hourly pay by five percent—then cut Bush's pay to $190,000. (The same principle should apply to congressmen and senators.)

Just watch how fast we'll get a law capping CEO pay along with a big rise in the minimum wage.

My proposal ought to come as music to the ears of Congressional Republicans. You remember, the guys who constantly argue that the U.S. should be run like a business. Most successful businesses do, in fact, tie executive compensation to company performance via stock options. And like most corporate execs, the president is invariably a rich man. He can well afford a few down years, especially when you throw in such tasty perks as free health care, transportation, gifts from foreign leaders, meals, security, gym facilities and a kick-ass retirement plan (Bush's current projected payoff, assuming he only serves a single term, will total $6.6 million)—not to mention post-retirement book deals and ethically dubious speaking tours.

Of course, it's also true that presidential inaction on the scandalous healthcare crisis facing ordinary Americans might become miraculously alleviated should the president suddenly be forced to submit his bills to some sleazy claims rejecter in Connecticut.

"No, I'm sorry, Mr. Bash. I'm afraid that we don't cover ruptured nasal blood vessels. If you read section 12.3(b) of your policy—"

"That was twenty-seven years ago! I'm calling about this weird glassy look in my eyes. When my pictures appear in the paper, I have red eyes, like a dog."

"Ophthalmology? You have to call department D-104. Please hold."

One chat like that and we'll have socialized medicine faster than you can say "Francois Mitterand."

Erasing Bush From History

There will never be the moment of agony. There will be no moment of "Oh God"... There'll never be a moment of the shudder brought about by the lack of confidence. There's never a moment of doubt as to the course taken. There just won't be. Everything will be measured by results. The victor is always right. History ascribes to the victor qualities that may or may not actually have been there. And similarly to the defeated.
> —Bush political advisor Karl Rove, January 2002

FEBRUARY 27, 2001—"Our long national nightmare is over," reassured Gerald Ford upon taking the presidential oath of office after Nixon's 1974 resignation.

Our long national nightmare, on the other hand, is just beginning.

Under occupation by a criminal gang of usurpers, political instability resulting from a botched election plunging the economy into a spiritual schism of unknown proportions, the Fourth Estate's credibility destroyed as it deliberately ignores the biggest—the only—story that matters, the American system of governance is in the midst of its greatest crisis of confidence since the Civil War.

Yet to read the paper or listen to the radio or watch TV or surf the Web, you'd never know that anything was wrong. If no one talks about the problem, maybe it'll just...go...away. Behold: Ostrich Nation.

For the first time in the history of the American republic, most Americans do not recognize the man residing at 1600 Pennsylvania Avenue as their legitimate president. And try as he might to act like one—proposing bills, giving speeches, bombing enemy nations—George W. Bush doesn't possess the strength of personality or the force of will to convince us otherwise. Oddly, Bush's authority relies on tolerant Democratic politicians and supposedly liberal journalists, all of whom fear that unmasking Bush as an emperor with no votes risks dismantling their own tenuous hold on whatever power they think they hold. If presidential elections result in illegitimate presidents, after all, the same can be said of congressional races. Eventually, all of the fictions that hold our society together—that we're all created equal, that a rectangular piece of paper printed with black and green ink is worth a dollar—could vaporize.

People questioning everything is called revolution. When the mob comes looking for your ass, it doesn't much matter if you're a wealthy white conservative corporate suck-up or a wealthy white liberal corporate suck-up— either way you end up twisting in the wind.

That's why Bush's would-be opponents are running scared.

But crises deferred are not crises departed. At some point during the next four to eight years, someone will dare to note that Bush is more Resident than President. In a perfect world this would happen sooner. Better yet that the Generalissimo would go back to executing Texas prison inmates, but our national predilection for procrastination makes it likely that in 2004 we'll undergo the farce of a reelection campaign for a guy who was never elected in the first place. Whether in 2005 or 2009 or 2013, some new Democrat—or, conceivably, a Republican—will determine whether the Y2K election fiasco culminates in sociopolitical implosion or allows the grand American experiment to continue.

First and foremost, the next legitimately elected president—assuming that our system can still produce such a creature—should upon assuming office sign an executive order invalidating all laws, executive orders and regulations passed during the illegal Bush regime. The Bush Residency, while a fascinating subject of political study, ought to be expunged from the official historical record. Because he was installed by a rogue Supreme Court in an illicit extraconstitutional maneuver, George W. Bush represents a grotesque detour from democracy. Accordingly, his name should be purged from lists of elected presidents, never to be immortalized by statues, images or his name on airports or schools.

Furthermore, the men and women who served as political appointees in the illegal Bush interregnum should be banned for life from government service. Their opportunism and vacuous cynicism hardly rises to the level of treason, but their singular lack of integrity—amply proven by working for a "president" who assumed power through sleazy back-door deals—must not be rewarded. This particularly includes Dick Cheney and members of Bush's pseudo-cabinet.

Finally, the five members of the Supreme Court who conspired to install an unelected Republican as president should be brought up on impeachment charges. Only a full Congressional investigation, with its accompanying scrupulous review of documents and eyewitnesses, can reveal exactly how and why these jurists abdicated their duty to the Constitution in such a transparently political ploy and whether any of them deserves to keep his or her job. The public deserves to know exactly what happened that fateful weekend the nation's highest court suspended the vote count in Florida. And they deserve to know it soon.

President Clinton's legitimate successor (who has, of course, yet to be elected) will face an enormous challenge. He (or she) will have to restore trust in democracy, the economic system and in America itself. It will be extraordinarily tempting to "just move on," in the popular parlance of the conservative idiots, and "get over it." History moves on but unaddressed problems fester with ever increasing malignancy the longer they're ignored. Wiping the slate clean is the only appropriate response to a presidency that never was and never should have been. Eradicating Bush from history would demonstrate respect for the law and an understanding of history, not to mention a maturing of our political process.

Naturally, there is no way that this will happen.

The Results Are In:
Gore Won Florida

The Miami Herald and USA Today reported that in most cases, Mr. Bush's narrow margin of victory would have held up if the court had allowed a hand recount of Florida ballots to continue. The newspapers reported that if the most inclusive standard were applied to undervotes on punch-card ballots, Mr. Bush's margin would have risen to 1,665 votes from the state-certified 537 votes. Under somewhat more restrictive standards, Mr. Bush still would have won the state by a few hundred votes. But under a much stricter standard for reviewing ballots, in which a hole next to a candidate's name had been marked cleanly through, the newspapers said, former Vice President Al Gore would have picked up enough votes to win by three votes.
—John M. Broder, The New York Times, April 5, 2001

APRIL 9, 2001—Now, finally, the results are in. Five months after Election Night, the *Miami Herald* and *USA Today* announced the results of their painstaking recount of Florida's controversial ballots: Bush won.

Well, not in reality. For one thing, the media recount includes neither Duval nor Holmes counties—two northern districts that refused to release their ballots for public inspection. Oh, and it ignores some 200,000 "undervotes"—ballots that supposedly contain no mark whatsoever; and 110,000 "overvotes"—those with marks for more than one candidate. And there's another problem. According to the *New York Times:* "In county after county, the number of ballots produced for the newspapers' examination of so-called undervotes...failed to match the totals reported by those counties in the immediate aftermath of the election last November." Some examples: 330 ballots disappeared from Orange County, 137 from Hillsborough and 67 from Pinellas. Out of 67 counties, 59 (!) "lost" votes.

Would someone please check Jeb's glove compartment?

Despite this "vote slippage," the newspapers pressed forward. The media recount of about 60,000 disputed ballots applied four different counting standards:

Clean-Punch: No hanging chads, just a clean hole for one candidate

Two-Corner: At least two corners are detached

Palm Beach: Dimpled chads—there's a bump but no detached corners—count only if there's more than one dimple

Most Inclusive: Any mark whatsoever counts as a vote

Then they further divided each of those four counts into two more: One for the sixty counties ordered recounted by the Florida Supreme Court on December 8, 2000 and another for all sixty-seven counties in the state.

Using the most conservative standard possible—clean-punch for only sixty counties—Gore won by three votes. Using the most liberal standard—Most Inclusive for all sixty-seven counties—Gore won by 393 votes. Bush only wins using counting scenarios his own campaign violently opposed and sued over; for example, he wins by 1,665 votes using the Most Inclusive standard for sixty counties. Nonetheless, the last week has seen the bizarre spectacle of Republican apologists crowing over "winning" by applying the very same standard they've been against all along.

Depending on the counting standard, the range of results falls between Gore by 393 to Bush by 1,665, meaning that a thousand-vote variance in either direction determines the outcome. But 330,000 over- and undervotes remain unconsidered, and thousands more have mysteriously disappeared. With a pool of *330 times* the number of disputed votes floating around, neither Bush nor Gore can be accurately called the victor of the Florida media recount.

Not that that stopped the Bushies. "President Bush was lawfully elected on Election Day. He won after the first statewide machine recount," announced Republican lawyer Mark Wallace in Miami. "He won after the manual recount, and he won at the conclusion of all the litigation."

Strictly speaking, Bush had little use for legality while plotting his December Surprise. Rather than push for the statewide recount that would have put questions of presidential illegitimacy to rest once and for all, Bush's posse arranged for his five GOP allies on the Supreme Court to stop the recount—a recount using a standard that, it now turns out, would have put Al Gore in the White House.

The cynical Bush was so desperate to "win" that he was willing to risk being considered illegitimate the next four to eight years if a media recount didn't prove him the victor after the fact.

Bear in mind: Even if Bush had won the recount, he would still not be the legit President of the United States. Bush was illegally installed by an outlaw Supreme Court determined to subvert the states' constitutional right to run elections. You don't get to call yourself legit unless you're willing to await the counting of the votes.

As it is, Bush's gamble came up snake eyes. That's why most Americans believe that the real president is teaching journalism at Columbia University right now. Whether or not you count the Palm Beach County Buchananites, Bush lost the race. Gore lost his will to fight. And we've lost our delusions of democracy.

The Triumph of Entropy

Built to withstand earthquakes and hurricane-force winds, and equipped with enhanced security after a 1993 terrorist bombing, the twin towers of New York's World Trade Center were supposed to last. Their architect boasted that they could withstand the impact of a jumbo jet. But when two hijacked commercial jetliners crashed into the 110-story structures within 15 minutes of each other early Tuesday morning, experts flinched, for "what we saw today was several orders of magnitude beyond anything we'd seen before," said the National Academy of Sciences' Richard Little, who has overseen several studies on how to protect buildings from terrorist attacks.

"We were hopeful at first," added Pennsylvania State University architectural engineer Kevin Parfitt, who teaches a course in building failures. "But the longer the fire burned, the more we feared the outcome."

The towers were built like "rectangular doughnuts," Parfitt said. Strength came from a central steel core and from steel columns spaced closely around the perimeter of each building. There was no structural support between the core and the outer walls. "When the planes come through, they cut through a number of those (perimeter) columns," Parfitt said. "At the same time, the planes are starting transcontinental flights, and they have full tanks of aviation fuel. You get a massive explosion and a fire."

—The Washington Post, September 12, 2001

SEPTEMBER 11, 2001—Images of iconic edifices flashed on the screen as my civil engineering professor clicked the forward button on his slide projector. The Parthenon. The Eiffel Tower. The Coliseum. The Hoover Dam. The Great Pyramid at Cheops.

The World Trade Center.

"What do all of these things have in common?" asked my instructor. My first guess would have been "they're all man-made," but I'd been in college for two whole years. In college, simple answers are always wrong, so I shut up. A hand shot up a few rows up.

"They're all man-made."

"Wrong. The common thread"—a slide of the White House, then of Stonehenge blinked by—"is that all of these things will eventually fall down."

47

"You mean, over time?" someone else asked.

"I mean, all of them will fall down. It's inevitable. It might be tomorrow or it might take ten thousand years. But it'll happen. The job of the structural engineer is twofold. First, to stave off the inevitable as long as you can. And second, never build anything so big that it will cause big problems when it comes down."

He used the Twin Towers as an example. "The World Trade Center ought never have been built," he told us back in September of 1983. "It has magnificent hanging-curtain construction. Its main support piles go forty floors down into solid bedrock. But it will fall down. And when it does, it will kill not only the forty thousand people who work there"— by 2001, the building population was closer to fifty thousand—"it will kill countless thousands of people in the buildings and streets around it."

I've never looked at those skyscrapers since without considering those words. About a year ago I strolled across the concrete plaza in front of the two buildings with a friend from Los Angeles. A security guard was hassling two skateboarders; I wonder if he made it home alive today. "They're just so huge," she noted. Not only was that one hundred ten story stack incomprehensibly high, each floor was individually massive. Office space in WTC was considered undesirable because the walk from the elevators to individual offices could add ten minutes to your round-trip commute. The place had its own zip code—10048—and it needed it. "Just consider," my Angeleno friend remembers me quoting my professor, "the mess that these things would make if they ever came down."

But most New Yorkers considered the World Trade Center indestructible. My wife was describing the suicide attacks on live television via cell phone as I sat on a New Jersey commuter train en route to Philadelphia. I relayed each twist and turn in the dramatic events of the day to my fellow passengers. All listened raptly until I reported that the first tower had imploded.

"No *way!*" my traveling companion scolded me. Several people turned away, convinced that I was talking shit. Damage, sure, but total collapse? That was impossible.

Any building can become a target, the victim of an accident or an act of God. But building on a grand scale not only escalates the potential death toll, it makes damage control exponentially more difficult. Ladders can't reach people stranded on the ninetieth floor. Firefighters can't drag heavy equipment up seventy five flights of stairs. Everyone knows that extremely tall structures can't be evacuated in the event of emergency. It's a grim trade-off: in exchange for the bragging rights to a dramatically tall structure, thousands of people tacitly risk their lives every day they show up for work. And if you place that huge edifice in the middle of one of the most densely populated urban centers on the planet, you risk thousands more on the surrounding streets.

It's like my professor said: Everything falls down sooner or later. If it hadn't been passenger jets commandeered by terrorists, it would have been something else. September 11 was inevitable. If anything, it could have been even worse—what if one or both towers had fallen over rather than vertically imploding?

As it is, the gap in the skyline is galling. Leaving that spot blank after the rubble has been carted away would be a concession to mass murderers. The World Trade Center ought to be rebuilt, bigger and taller than ever, as a testament to the indomitable American spirit embodied by New York itself. We too often forget that symbolism is important, but let's rebuild this thing.

Never forget, though. Whatever we build, someday it too will fall.

After 9/11, a Right-Wing Power Grab

Ordinarily when the president of the United States addresses a joint session of Congress, the leaders of the opposition party give a statement, and they respond. Tonight there is no opposition party. We stand here united, not as Republicans and Democrats, not as Southerners or Westerners or Midwesterners or Easterners, but as Americans. I guess there are those in the world that thought this would pull us apart. We would start blaming each other, and we wouldn't come to each other's aid.
— *Trent Lott, Senate Minority Leader (R-MI), September 20, 2001*

SEPTEMBER 25, 2001—We've been treated to some astonishingly vile images over the last two weeks: office workers hurling themselves into a hundred-floor-high abyss. A gaping, smoldering hole in the financial center of our greatest city. George W. Bush passing himself off as a patriot, even as he disassembles the Constitution with the voracious glee of jackals ripping out the innards of a fallen wildebeest.

"There is no opposition party," Republican Congressional leader Trent Lott chillingly announced as Democratic counterpart Tom Daschle watched in silent, cowed assent after Bush's speech to a joint session of Congress. And even if it's mainly the result of our pathetic desire to follow someone—anyone—in the aftermath of September 11, there's little opposition out in the cities and towns across our vast continent. Bush's job approval rating is hovering up there with puppies and sunny days.

"War" was declared against America on September 11, Bush told us, and we're declaring "war" right back. War against whom? Afghanistan? Iraq? Canada? One can declare war against a nation-state, not against terrorists living inside a country. You can ask a foreign government to extradite accused terrorists for trial, but you're not likely to get very far if you don't share good diplomatic relations. And according to the Constitution, the President—even an illegitimate president—doesn't declare war. Congress does.

Without so much as an invocation of the Constitution-bending War Powers Act—which would allow the President to commit troops for a limited time—here we are at "war." Troops are being mobilized and allies are being gathered to fight...whomever. Whatever. Wherever. Wallowing in a level of cynicism unseen since Lyndon Johnson conned Congress into a Vietnam War based on a Tonkin Gulf incident that never happened, Bush has capi-

talized on a nation's grief, confusion and anger to extort a political blank check payable in young American blood.

First we have to "get"—read, murder—alleged terrorist mastermind and perennial bugaboo Osama bin Laden. If we're willing to play by the rules, we may be able to convince the Taliban government of Afghanistan to turn him over. "We rule out the possibility of his handover to America without substantial evidence," Taliban spokesman Abdul Hai Mutmaen said September 24. Although this demand is nothing more than any country, not least the United States, would insist upon before extradition, the Bushies disdainfully refer to this adherence to basic international law as "a stalling tactic." But even if you don't believe that the Afghan government deserves this courtesy after all they've done (whatever that is), how about us? After all, we live—or lived, before the Supreme Court subverted it last December—in a democracy. Aren't we entitled to see definitive proof tying Osama bin Laden and/or the Taliban to the hijack attacks before we send our sons and daughters off to die in the Hindu Kush? Shouldn't we exhaust all the possibilities of diplomacy before resorting to military force?

When President John F. Kennedy wanted to convince the American public of his claims, he went on television to show us surveillance photos of Soviet missiles in Cuba. Television cameras followed troops into battle in Vietnam. But according to an anonymous defense official, this government doesn't believe that it's beholden to the people. "There is a new way of doing business here, and it's not in the sunshine." And the "war" itself will be waged far away from prying journalists. "It may include dramatic strikes visible on TV and covert operations—secret even in success," smirks Bush.

We're at war with whomever Bush decides is our enemy. Not only won't he tell us how

or why they're our enemies, he won't tell us how or why we're attacking them, or how or why our citizens are getting killed trying to do it. Welcome to 'cause-I-said-so-ocracy.

"It's important as this war progresses that the American people understand we make decisions based upon classified information, and we will not jeopardize the sources," Bush arrogantly announced. "We will not make the war more difficult to win by publicly disclosing classified information."

For a guy who hired goons to physically threaten Florida election officials, Bush is asking for an awful lot of trust in his one-man crusade against the Muslim world. Let's get this straight. We're supposed to believe this guy's account of "classified" information—even while he tells us that, from now on, he'll be lying to us for our own good?

If ever there was a classic naked emperor moment, it was the morning after Bush's address to Congress. A competently delivered committee-written hack job was breathlessly equated by projecting liberals and conservatives alike with the soaring oratorical highlights of FDR and Winston Churchill. Such is our craving for leadership that we're anointing a doltish daddy's boy who still refuses to come clean about his DWI record with the mandate of heaven. Pacifism is no way to run a superpower. If concrete proof can be presented that a group or individual directly participated in the massacre of thousands of New Yorkers and Washingtonians, those people deserve to be brought to justice or killed in the attempt to apprehend them. I, for one, would shed no tears for the inhuman scum who caused so much misery to so many. But the memories of our dead will be poorly served if we let right-wing extremists bring about the imperial presidency Bush is shoving down our throats. Blank-check democracy, if you stop to think about it, is no democracy at all.

But who's got time to think?

Drop the Bomb

"We have taken every possible step to avoid civilian casualties, to make sure that the U.S. military response is carefully targeted...This is, as we have made clear many, many times, not an attack on the Afghan people. The objective is to end the terrorist threat to the world community."

—*Richard Boucher, Department of State spokesman,*
October 11, 2001

OCTOBER 16, 2001—Beware collateral damage, for today's hey-nothing-personal victims give rise to tomorrow's terrorists. As this goes to press, a bestiary of bombs—a few five hundred pounders here, some "bunker busters" there—is falling on Afghan cities. Bombing, despite laughable assertions to the contrary, is anything but a precision art. Bombs go off-course. Bombs hit things that themselves blow up and kill people who weren't supposed to die. Civilians hang out where they shouldn't. And information about bombing targets is often plain wrong or out of date.

The bottom line is this: Ordinary Afghans, men and women and children who have never done anything wrong to anyone, are being mangled and killed by American bombs. The innocents have spouses, parents and friends, and these spouses, parents and friends quite naturally have a tendency to dislike those who mangled and killed their loved ones. Their hatred festers. Some of them will eventually come to be persuaded that vengeance will soothe their pain. And one day they'll fly planes into office buildings or blow themselves up in shopping malls or do something as yet unimaginable.

Getting even doesn't do much good if our vengeance only creates more terrorism.

And yet the right-wingers are absolutely correct when they assert that doing nothing is not a viable option. Whether we had September 11 coming or not, giving peace a chance is a supreme act of self-denial: there is no peace. Whether or not the victims cry for vengeance is moot. No nation is worthy of the name unless it's willing to react to the murder of its citizens with force. Bush is, like it or not, doing something. People respect that, even if that something later turns out to be counterproductive.

There is, however, an intelligent middle ground between the commonly considered binary of mindless bombing versus mindless pacifism. Neither liberal nor conservative, a thoughtful solution can be found by applying what we Americans do so well during peacetime: simple common sense.

Bush's "war on terrorism" is, like previous wars on drugs and poverty, too vague and neb-

PALESTINIAN DEMONSTRATORS SHOCKED AMERICAN TV VIEWERS BY CELEBRATING THE PLANE ATTACKS ON THE WORLD TRADE CENTER AND THE PENTAGON.

WHAT TH-? WHY DO THEY **HATE** US SO MUCH?

I'D GO TO DISNEYWORLD IF IT WASN'T IN AMERICA!

WHY ON EARTH WOULD ANYONE, LEAST OF ALL MUSLIMS, HAVE A PROBLEM WITH LITTLE OL' US? AFTER ALL, WE TREAT OTHERS WITH NOTHING BUT RESPECT.

OUTTA MY WAY, FRICKIN' **DOT!**

ALL TOWELHEADS AND CAMEL JOCKEYS MUST **DIE!**

SURE, WE BOMB IRAQ SO OFTEN THAT IT'S NOT NEWS. SURE, WE BLEW UP A SUDANESE ASPIRIN PLANT WITHOUT BOTHERING TO APOLOGIZE. SURE, WE FINANCE AN ISRAEL THAT STEALS PALESTINIANS' LAND, BULLDOZES THEIR HOMES, TORTURES AND STARVES THEM TO DEATH.

HALT

WE DON'T GIVE THE MISERY WE CAUSE A SECOND THOUGHT. NO WONDER WE'RE SO DAMNED SURPRISED.

WHY DOES AMERICA HATE US **SO** MUCH?

©2001 TED RALL

ulous to win. Our first priority ought to be to bring remaining perpetrators, if any, of the attacks on the Pentagon and World Trade Center to justice; if they end up dead in the attempt to arrest them so be it.

Second, while we'll never eradicate terrorist attacks on American soil, we can minimize their number and their intensity when they do occur. This requires a delicate combination of force and tact. We must be kind as well as forceful.

Afghanistan's Taliban regime is at best indirectly involved with the September 11th hijackings. (The Bush Administration admits that it couldn't indict Osama or the Taliban based on the evidence it currently possesses.) Forget the passports: eighteen out of the nineteen hijackers were ethnic Egyptian; one was Saudi. The smart money points to one of the Middle East's most venerable militant Islamic organizations, Gama'at al-Islamiyya, or the Islamic Group. Founded by Sheikh Omar Abdel Rahman, currently serving a life sentence for the 1993 World Trade Center bombing, Gama'at al-Islamiyya is best known for the November 1997 massacre of sixty-two tourists at the Temple of Luxor in Egypt and the assassination of Egyptian President Anwar Sadat in 1981. Though the Islamic Group is composed of numerous splinter cells whose ideology varies, they share a common aim: the replacement of the secular Egyptian government of Hosni Mubarak by an Islamic theocracy. The Islamic Group resents the U.S. for propping up the Mubarak government as much as Israel.

Egyptians are, according to most reports, the main suspects for September 11. Others point to Saudi Arabia, particularly on the funding front. So why are we attacking Afghanistan? American intelligence should work with the Egyptian government to track down members of Gama'at al-Islamiyya associated with the New York and Washington attacks and put them on trial for mass murder. Arresting murderers ought to take precedence over bombing the places where they trained.

A targeted approach would demonstrate to all but the most fanatic elements in the Arab world that the United States is a nation whose retribution takes place after fair, measured consideration. It would also serve to destroy the one Islamist network to have drawn the most American blood—and reduce the odds of a repeat performance.

Though we should continue providing economic and military assistance to Israel, that aid ought to be predicated on several conditions. First, in conformity with United Nations resolutions, all Israeli settlements in the Palestinian territories ought to be shut down and evacuated. Second, Israel should guarantee an end to its more egregious human rights abuses, such as the demolition of Arab homes and rocket attacks on civilian targets. Finally, internal border blockades of Gaza and the West Bank should be permanently halted. This bilateral policy—supporting Israel while refusing to tolerate religious apartheid—would show that we stand behind our friends but only to the extent that they behave in a civilized manner. Best of all, it would end an absurd state of affairs in which a superpower is repeatedly manipulated by a resource-free desert nation the size of New Jersey.

We should drop sanctions and military action against such nations as Iraq and Afghanistan in exchange for verifiable assurances that neither country harbor terrorists who target the United States. Then we should pour in humanitarian assistance to show ordinary Muslims that Americans care about their plight. Let a co-opted postwar Taliban root out al-Qaeda and other groups within their territory; it's a hell of a lot easier to let the locals do our dirty work than to send in American ground troops.

But first, let's stop this stupid bombing.

The New McCarthyism

Despite numerous demonstrations of patriotism and unity across the country following the terrorist attacks, America's college campuses are running rampant with anti-American and anti-capitalism sentiment. The antiwar movement is embarking upon a nostalgic binge that ignores the committed terrorist attacks on American civilians. Professors are leading radical left-wing students in a campaign to attack America's sacred institutions of capitalism and civic duty, and student columnists are serving as daily catalysts for anti-American sentiment.
—*Young Americans for Freedom press release, October 31, 2001*

NOVEMBER 6, 2001—According to the *Wall Street Journal*, I'm "probably the most bitterly anti-American commentator in America." *The National Review* calls me "a big fat zero, an ignorant, talentless hack with a flair for recycling leftist pieties into snarky cartoons that inspired breakfast-table chuckles among the leftist literati and the granola-munching types." It's not just conservatives who have taken a bead on me: The *New Republic* cites my work in its regular "Idiocy Watch" section.

What have I done to merit such bipartisan vitriol, most of it in publications that have always ignored me? Here's what: since September 11, I've written eight columns and drawn twenty-four editorial cartoons examining various aspects of that fateful morning and its aftermath. Some of my pieces expressed pain and anger at the murder of thousands of innocent people. Others sought, sometimes humorously and sometimes not, to answer the widely asked question "Why do they hate us so much?" I've taken the Bush Administration to task for cynical manipulation of a national crisis to promote partisan political agenda items such as drilling in the Arctic, fast-track authority on free trade and eliminating the alternative minimum tax. And I've also pointed out to Americans that the Administration's war against the Taliban may have something to do with the potential profitability of the Trans-Afghanistan pipeline project between the Caspian and Arabian Seas.

Like all New Yorkers, I grieve for the dead and remain shocked by the magnitude of our loss. But I still have the same job to do as I had back in August. I'm paid to express my ideas and opinions. And my opinions still include the firmly held belief that President Bush was illegally installed via a judicial coup d'état. I honestly think that our bombing of Afghanistan is misguided and hypocritical. And I still believe in a freedom-loving America where opposing opinions don't vanish in the glare of a 93 percent popularity rating. Although some of

my fellow political cartoonists have taken to mocking all things Arab, toeing the official Pentagon line, and cranking out brain-addled propaganda, I've continued to skewer the President and his policies. I consider it my patriotic duty to do so.

Insulting American politicians and American policies doesn't make one anti-American. It makes one an integral part of the American process.

War brings out the best and worst in a society, a truism that is just as apt here at home as it is on the battlefield. I've always received hate mail—such is the price one pays for publicly expressing any strong opinion—but in recent weeks the level of hatred—why do they hate me so much?—has escalated to include frighteningly credible death threats. People who might have advised me to engage in self-coitus prior to September 11th now demand that I commit suicide, using the most disturbing language imaginable. Readers who once threatened to cancel their newspaper subscriptions because they took offense at something I wrote or drew now threaten to contact advertisers in a concerted effort to, as one e-mailer put it, "make sure that you never work again and die homeless in the gutter." My mother, living in a bellwether county in Ohio and perhaps more in touch with mainstream America than I, is worried. "I'm afraid that you'll lose your job," she warns, urging me to be less critical of the Republicans.

She, like me, has never experienced anything quite like this before.

Oh, and my phone is probably tapped. It began a few weeks ago. They did a crummy job; even when my computer is off, the external modem emits a loud dial tone. You can hear some idiot whispering, "Is he talking or has he hung up?" My faxes drive them nuts. I hope that the government's efforts to locate Osama bin Laden are being carried out with more finesse than this low-budget assault on my civil rights. The feds, I assume, are merely fol-

lowing up White House spokesman Ari Fleischer's chilling warning that Americans ought to watch what they say and what they do. I've done neither, nor do I intend to.

The war on terrorism, it seems, requires us not only to zip our nail clippers and Swiss Army knives into check-in luggage but also to zip our lips. There's a new atmosphere of hyperconformity where nothing less than total alignment with the White House is currently acceptable. Bill Maher, the libertarian host of *Politically Incorrect*, has enthusiastically supported the Bush Administration's war against Afghanistan. Nonetheless, a politically incorrect remark about the semantics of cowardice looks like it's about to cause ABC television to cancel his show.

We're living in dangerous times, and this neo-McCarthyist trend toward blacklists, the silencing of dissent, and government attacks on personal freedom represent an even greater threat to our country than terrorism. Nothing, after all, is more fundamentally un-American than keeping your mouth shut.

I Can See Clearly Now
the Pain is Gone

President Bush announced today the appointment of Dr. Zalmay Khalilzad as his Special Presidential Envoy for Afghanistan. The Special Envoy is a representative to the Afghan people as they seek to consolidate a new order, reconstruct their country and free it from al-Qaeda and Taliban control. The position of the Special Envoy was established to underscore the President's support for these objectives. He will report to the President through Secretary of State Colin Powell. Dr. Khalilzad will continue as the Special Assistant to the President for Southwest Asia, Near East and North Africa, reporting through the National Security Advisor, Dr. Condoleezza Rice.

—The White House, December 31, 2001

JANUARY 8, 2002—Conspiracy theories are funny things: the wackier they sound, the more likely they are to be true. The fires of September were still burning when I, among others, suggested that the Bush regime's Afghan war might have more to do with old-fashioned oil politics than bringing the Evil Ones to justice.

Little did I know how quickly I would be proven right.

The Taliban government and their al-Qaeda "guests," after all, both were at best bit players in the terror biz. If the U.S. had really wanted to dispatch a significant number of jihad boys to meet the black-eyed virgins, it would have bombed Pakistan instead of Afghanistan. Instead, the State Department inexplicably cozied up to this snake pit of anti-American extremists, choosing a nation led by a dictator who seized power in an illegal coup as our principal South Asian ally.

Moreover, the American military strategy in Afghanistan—dropping bombs without inserting a significant number of ground troops—all but guaranteed that Osama would live to kill another day.

So the Third Afghan War obviously isn't about fighting terrorism. This leads certain hardboiled cynics to conclude that it must be about (yawwwwwwn) oil. Bush and Cheney are both former oil company execs, after all, and National Security Advisor Condoleezza Rice was corporate counsel at Chevron. Unbeknownst to most Americans, oil fields dot northern Afghanistan near its border with Turkmenistan. But the real jackpot is under the

Caspian Sea. Between confirmed and estimated oil reserves, Kazakhstan may be destined to become the world's largest oil-producing nation, a bonanza that is expected to dwarf even the vast reserves of Saudi Arabia within a few years.

For the U.S., more production means cheaper oil, lower production and transportation costs, and higher corporate profits. The Kazakhs would be happy to work out a pipeline deal with us, but their oil is frustratingly landlocked. The shortest and cheapest of all possible pipelines would run from the Caspian to the Persian Gulf via Iran, but lingering American diplomatic tension from the 1980 hostage crisis has prevented U.S.-aligned Kazakhstan from getting its crude out to sea using that route. Plan B is a 1996-era Unocal scheme for a Trans-Afghanistan pipeline that would debouch near the Arabian Sea port of Karachi.

As Zalmay Khalilzad co-wrote in the *Washington Quarterly* for its Winter 2000 issue, "Afghanistan could prove a valuable corridor for this [Caspian Sea] energy as well as for access to markets in Central Asia." Khalilzad has an unsavory past. As a State and Defense Department official during the Reagan years, Khalilzad helped supply the anti-Soviet *mujahadeen*—their alumni may have helped plan 9/11—with weapons they're now using to fight Americans. During the 1990s, he worked as Unocal's chief consultant on its Afghan pipeline scheme.

According to the French daily *Libération*, Khalilzad's $200 million project was originally conceived to run 830 miles from Dauletabad in southeastern Turkmenistan across Afghanistan to Multan, Pakistan because Multan already possesses a link to Karachi. Partly on Khalilzad's advice, the Clinton Administration indirectly funded the Taliban via the ISI Pakistani intelligence agency, going so far as to pay the salaries of high-ranking Taliban officials. Their goal: a strong, stable authoritarian regime in Kabul to ensure the safety of

Unocal's precious crude oil.

In 1998, after Taliban "guest" Osama bin Laden bombed two American embassies in East Africa, Unocal shelved the plan due to political unfeasibility. Chief consultant Khalilzad moved on to the Rand Corporation think tank. Concluding that the Taliban were irredeemably unreliable, Clinton withdrew U.S. support from the pipeline deal. But as a newly minted cliché goes, everything changed after 9/11. Now the Taliban are gone, replaced by a U.S.-installed interim government, and good business is where you find it.

Rising energy prices helped push the economy into recession; perhaps ninety-cent gas will work where interest rate cuts failed. Once again, the pipeline plan is hot.

Did Bush exploit the September 11 attacks in order to justify a Central Asian oil grab? The answer seems clear. On December 31, 2001, Bush appointed his first special envoy to Afghanistan: Zalmay Khalilzad. "This is a moment of opportunity for Afghanistan," the former Unocal employee commented upon arrival in Kabul on January 5. You bet it is: Pakistan's *Frontier Post* reports that U.S. Ambassador Wendy Chamberlain met with Pakistan's oil minister to discuss reviving the Unocal project in October during the first few days of the war against Afghanistan.

And a front-page story in the January 9 *New York Times* reveals that "the United States is preparing a military presence in Central Asia that could last for years," including building a permanent air base in the Kyrgyz Republic, formerly part of the Soviet Union. (The Bushies say that they just want to keep an eye on postwar Afghanistan, but few students of the region buy their explanation.) Many industry experts consider Unocal's revived Afghan adventure fatally flawed and expect the U.S. to ultimately wise up and pursue a deal with Iran. But thus far the Bushies have given the conspiracy theorists a lot to think about.

A Government of Gangsters

Vice President Dick Cheney and Defense Secretary Donald H. Rumsfeld said today that the war captives in Afghanistan and Guantánamo Bay, Cuba, would not be designated as prisoners of war, regardless of what decision the administration made on Secretary of State Colin L. Powell's request for a review of how the Geneva Convention on captives' rights might apply.

Secretary Powell agrees that the captives should not be given prisoner of war status, but he has asked the administration to reconsider whether to adhere to the Geneva Convention governing treatment of prisoners in wartime, adopted in 1949. Mr. Cheney said the convention did not apply to those captives because they were not conventional soldiers, but terrorists operating outside internationally accepted norms.

Reflecting a debate within the administration, Mr. Cheney told Fox News this morning that the question was whether the prisoners should be treated within the confines of the convention or outside it. He prefers the latter course because it would allow flexibility in interrogation. "There's another school of thought that says the Geneva Convention does not apply to terrorist attacks," Mr. Cheney said. "It was set up to deal with a war between sovereign states. It's got provisions for dealing with civil war. But in a case where you have nonstate actors out to kill civilians, then there's a serious question whether or not the Geneva Convention even applies.

"The bottom line is that the legal issue is being debated between the lawyers. It will go to the president. He'll make a decision."
—Katharine Q. Seelye, New York Times, January 28, 2002

JANUARY 29, 2002—Unbridled legal hypocrisy is a recurring tactic of the ideologically impoverished Bush imperium. When it suits their immediate aims, the Bushies wield the law like a club. As soon as the niceties of legal process prove inconvenient, however, they chuck the U.S. Code out the window like a discarded gum wrapper.

We've seen this schizy lurching back and forth between law-and-order conservatism and anarchic retro-Tricky Dicky Nixonism since November 2000, when the same campaign that sued under Florida's election laws to stop that state's ballot recount resorted to

hired thugs and backroom deals when it became obvious that they were going to lose.

Born illegitimately of intimidation, this administration is waging its New War on Terror with the same graceless style it used to seize power. Before 9/11, Bush relied upon international organizations and legal strictures to impose economic sanctions on Afghanistan. As the Trade Center towers burned and Bush's polls soared, the new century's Reichstag Fire had the usual effect. The last vestige of respect for law vanished. Bush dropped bombs without declaring war, without bothering to formally request that the Taliban extradite Osama bin Laden, and without presenting a smidgen of proof that either the Afghan government or bin Laden had anything to do with the attacks on New York and Washington. "You're either with us or against us," Bush belched. In the lexicon of this band of gangsters, "us" means "me."

During the last several months, at least six thousand people have vanished off the streets of the United States. Kidnapped by government agents, they have no idea when—or if—they will be released from prison. Bush Administration officials claim that these presumed detainees overstayed their visas, that they have links to al-Qaeda, that they don't wash their hands after using the toilet, that America is safer because they're behind bars. Is any of this true? Who knows? Since the disappeared haven't been granted access to lawyers or allowed to call their families, no can talk to them. Bush says they have no rights because they're not American citizens-but we don't even know if that's true.

Keep that in mind the next time you travel abroad. If we can do it to others, they can do it to us.

Granted, the Bush police state doesn't coddle its own citizens. John Walker Lindh, an American with the bad taste to join the Taliban and the worse luck to get caught without

firing a shot, was held for weeks without even being told that his parents had hired him an attorney. You may or may not give a damn about Walker. That's your right. Since he's an American citizen accused of serious federal crimes, however, what happens to his rights happens to yours. The fact that he's been denied legal counsel, that Attorney General John Ashcroft's outrageous statements to the media have made it impossible for him to get a fair trial, and that Bush previously considered subjecting him to one of his kangaroo court military tribunals, tells you everything Americans need to know about our leaders' respect for the law.

Don't deign to look down on Burma or North Korea; when it comes to human rights, you live in a rogue state, just like the citizens of those dictatorships. Exhibit A: The Taliban and accused al-Qaeda prisoners of war now being held in unsheltered dog pens at the U.S. marine base at Guantánamo Bay, Cuba. Despite European criticism of the conditions under which they are being held, Dick Cheney insists that "nobody should feel defensive or unhappy about the quality of treatment they've received." Maybe so. But if our government has nothing to be ashamed of, why can't reporters, lawyers or family members get inside to visit them?

Even more troubling is the administration's assertion that these men are "unlawful combatants" not entitled to the decent living conditions and other protections guaranteed by the Geneva Convention. When Nazi Germany executed captured soldiers of the French Resistance using the argument Bush now cites, the world was rightfully appalled. The Taliban prisoners' status is far clearer than the irregular *maquis*—the Afghans were an organized militia fighting to defend their own nation's government from an invading army. The Taliban, who controlled ninety-five percent of Afghanistan, were recognized as its government by three U.S.-aligned nations. If the Talibs aren't prisoners of war, who are?

Fortunately, the Geneva Convention addresses the current situation. In the event of a dispute over the status of prisoners, the agreement stipulates that "such prisoners shall enjoy the protection of the present convention until such time as their status has been determined by a competent tribunal." But, protests Cheney, "These detainees are the worst of a very bad lot. They are very dangerous. These are bad people. They may well have information about future terrorist attacks against the United States. We need that information. We need to be able to interrogate them and extract from them whatever information they have."

Vice President Klaus Barbie wants to torture our prisoners to get information that may or may not exist, that may or may not be useful. In his view, this justifies our making an end-run around one of the most important international agreements ever signed.

"The debate is not actually whether these people are prisoners of war," an anonymous State Department official told the *New York Times* on January 28, 2002. "They are not. The debate is why they are not prisoners of war." Cheney summed up the Bush position the next day: "They are not P.O.W.s. They will not be determined to be P.O.W.s." The fix is in.

To hear these loons tell it, the Geneva Convention exists solely to protect the safety and dignity of American servicemen when they fall into enemy hands. When we capture foreigners in combat, on the other hand, we simply claim that they're "unlawful combatants." Unfortunately for future American P.O.W.s—er, "detainees"—the rest of the world is listening closely.

After 9/11, many Americans wondered aloud why other citizens of the world hate us so much. What kind of actions could we or our government have undertaken that would explain such fury at little old us? Here's one example.

Everybody Must Get Stoned: The Kinder, Gentler Afghanistan

"In this country all law comes from Islam."
—*Judge Ahamat Ullha Zarif, January 28, 2002*

FEBRUARY 5, 2002—"In four short months," George W. Bush reported in his State of the Union address, "our nation has comforted the victims; begun to rebuild New York and the Pentagon; rallied a great coalition; captured, arrested, and rid the world of thousands of terrorists; destroyed Afghanistan's terrorist training camps; saved a people from starvation; and freed a country from brutal oppression."

Not quite.

The victims of 9/11 will be mourning and litigating for years to come. Not only is New York not rebuilding, it's watching its corporate tax base scurry off to suburbia as the Bush Administration brazenly welshes on its pledge to help the city with a much-needed $20 billion relief package Bush's coalition is a gathering of *real* evildoers, like Pakistan and Saudi Arabia, that fund and arm anti-American Islamic extremists. The United States is no closer to apprehending Osama bin Laden, Mullah Mohammad Omar or their henchmen than we were back in September.

"The last time we met in this chamber," Bush crowed, "the mothers and daughters of Afghanistan were captives in their own homes, forbidden from working or going to school."

In all the ways that matter, they still are. Afghan women continue to wear the all-encompassing *burqa*, infamous symbol of Taliban oppression, out of fear of reprisals and terror of being raped by heavily armed Northern Alliance soldiers running willy-nilly through the cities and countryside. For the same reasons, women rarely go outdoors. Few schools have money to hire teachers. Women may be legally allowed to work in Kabul, anyway but Afghanistan's male unemployment rate exceeds ninety-five percent. If and when economic activity resumes, male-run Afghanistan will take care of the old boys club first.

Nothing has changed in Afghanistan, simply because there has been no meaningful attempt to de-Talibanize the nation. Infamous figures like Mullah Omar are in hiding, but today's Northern Alliance-dominated regime is almost entirely comprised of Taliban defectors. So while prime minister Hamid Karzai cuts a dashing figure with his green Tajik robe and impeccable English, the soldier-goons ordinary Afghans come into contact with on the streets are merely gussied-up Talibs. Some liberation.

Nothing symbolized the excesses of Taliban rule more than that government's orgy of

Friday afternoon stonings and amputations. "Our Islam is different [from that]," Justice Minister Abdul Rahim Karimi, who took office on December 24, 2001, told *Agence France Presse*. Yet the Taliban's Sharia law—a pastiche of Pashtun tribal traditions and fundamentalist interpretations of the Koran that served in place of a modern Afghan legal system—remains in full force. "People would not understand if we got rid of it," Karimi explained.

Judge Ahamat Ullha Zarif, a leading Northern Alliance jurist, described justice in the kinder, gentler Afghanistan bought and paid for by you, the American taxpayer: "There will be some changes from the time of the Taliban," Zarif announced. "For example, the Taliban used to hang the victim's body in public for four days. We will only hang the body for a short time, say fifteen minutes."

People who have sex outside marriage—this includes unmarried couples—will continue to be stoned under Northern Alliance rule. "But we will use only small stones," he noted. Smaller stones offer the condemned the chance to escape. "If they are able to run away, they are free." As in America, this new soft-on-crime approach is contingent on cooperation and remorse. "Those who refuse to confess their wrongdoing and are condemned by a judge will have their hands and feet bound so that they cannot run away," Zarif went on. "They will certainly be stoned to death."

The good news for Afghans, such as it is, is that Sharia may assume a mellower form in some provinces. As law and order has vanished, a new civil war has fragmented the country into separate fiefdoms controlled by vicious U.S.-armed warlords. At the checkpoint separating the Abdul Hai Neamati and Ismail Khan sectors of Farah province in western Afghanistan, for example, each side flies a different Afghan flag. But both are equally committed to the identical core value—the joy of robbing and raping ordinary people.

Afghanistan's New Agony

LALAZHA, AFGHANISTAN—The man they knew in this hard-scrabble village as Tall Man Khan never had much in his life but his height, and even that was only about 5-feet-11. Then, early this month, he was killed in an American attack on what the Pentagon described as a group of people suspected of being leaders of al-Qaeda. American government officials said one of the people in the group was tall and was being treated with deference by those around him. That gave rise to speculation that the attack might have been directed at Osama bin Laden, who is 6-feet-4.

The American attack took the form of a Hellfire missile fired from a pilotless Predator drone operated by the C.I.A. It left bereaved wives and children, in an incident that may turn out to be a parable of what can happen when human error creeps into the use of remotely fired weaponry. It is also a warning, many Afghans say, that errant bombing and missile strikes by the United States may squander the overwhelming appreciation that America earned among 20 million Afghans when it forced the Taliban and its ally, al-Qaeda, from power.

—John F., Burns, New York Times, February 17, 2002

FEBRUARY 19, 2002—I realized that the United States was in trouble back in November 2001, when I spent three weeks in Afghanistan. Despite the Niagara-scale deluge of propaganda assuring Americans that thousands of indiscriminately dropped bombs would keep them safe from terrorism, the bloodbath I witnessed told me otherwise.

If anything, things have gotten worse since my trip.

On the subject of bombing, the lessons of military history are clear. No war has ever been won by bombing alone. And in almost every historical precedent, the hearts and minds of civilians turn against the side that bombs them. Partly this phenomenon is caused by "collateral damage"—people killed because they happen to be near a legitimate military target. What's made things worse in Afghanistan is that we've killed thousands of people by bombing villages and cities where no one had seen a Talib or al-Qaeda fighter in years. We've already killed more civilians than died in the 9/11 attacks—and as we know firsthand from that horrible day, watching innocent people killed creates rage among their survivors and fellow citizens.

To the Afghans, we're the terrorists. Someday we will pay a terrible price for killing their husbands, wives, sons and daughters. It's inevitable.

Trying to win through bombing was stupid. Bombing a country we knew nothing about was insane. The United States only committed approximately ten thousand ground troops to the war in Afghanistan, a country the size of Texas. Moreover, the few soldiers that we sent over are holed up at local airports and camps in the middle of the desert. U.S. troops occasionally venture out of their cantonments in SUVs with tinted windows for sit-downs with local warlords, but they rarely talk to the locals to find out what's really going on.

The interim government led by American puppet leader and former Unocal oil employee Hamid Karzai is impotent and incompetent; individual fiefdoms have sprung up all over Afghanistan to fill the power vacuum left by the fall of the Taliban. Fierce battles have broken out between the warlords of Herat and Kandahar, as well as those ruling Jalalabad and Khost. In one recent incident, Afghanistan's new aviation and tourism minister was stripped and stabbed to death as eight hundred Muslim pilgrims looked on at the Kandahar airport; Karzai blames his own intelligence and defense chiefs for the murder.

Afghanistan is not in danger of disintegrating into civil war. Civil war is well underway.

George W. Bush has two choices. He can order a withdrawal and let the Afghans fight it out amongst themselves. Pulling out, however, would mean admitting defeat—bad politics during a midterm election year. Alternatively, Bush could insert overwhelming numbers of American and allied coalition ground troops to sweep across the country, crush the warlords and impose unified military government. This would finish the job and get us out sooner. It would also help the Afghans. The trouble is, Bush prefers destroying nations to building them.

So his Administration has been choosing sides—and the consequences have been disastrous.

The enemy of my enemy is my friend, but there's an oft-ignored corollary: the friend of my enemy is my enemy. The U.S. is arming and funding Kandahar warlord Gul Agha and thuggish Jalalabad kingpin Haji Abdul Qadir in return for information about al-Qaeda fugitives. Both men have already turned those U.S.-supplied arms against rival commanders.

In the first major incident of civilian casualties to receive widespread attention from the international media, at least twenty-one innocent Afghan civilians were killed and twenty-seven arrested and brutally beaten in a botched U.S. raid on Khas Uruzgan in the Hazar Qadam valley north of Kandahar on January 21. "We were all sleeping. They didn't give us a chance to surrender," survivor Niaz Mohammed told the Associated Press. "They came to kill us." After repeated denials, the Central Intelligence Agency was finally forced to admit that it had been duped by a warlord, who used us to attack a rival. The detainees were released and the CIA issued thousand dollar payments to the families of the dead.

In December another warlord told U.S. forces that a convoy driving through Paktia province was carrying Taliban fighters. They were actually pro-Northern Alliance tribal elders who were on their way to Karzai's inauguration. American bombs killed "dozens," including many women and children accompanying the delegation.

"It takes an enormous amount of time [to develop trustworthy local agents] and you have to vet them against facts you know to be true," warns ex-CIA officer Robert Baer. "Because the Afghans are such a contentious people, they're always fighting, they're always out to get their neighbor across the other valley. So it's a treacherous situation and the more innocents we kill the more trouble we're going to get, the more likely that people are going to take revenge against our troops...It's a quagmire."

9/11 Changed Nothing

Preliminary analysis by the FBI showed the sneakers worn Saturday by a passenger on a trans-Atlantic flight from Paris to Miami contained "two functional improvised explosive devices," federal authorities said Sunday. U.S. authorities Sunday charged the passenger, Richard C. Reid, 28, with interfering with the performance of the duties of flight crew members by assault or intimidation. Meanwhile, the Federal Aviation Administration announced Sunday all U.S. airports are required to add random shoe checks of passengers to the already established practice of random baggage checks. The FAA warned airlines earlier this month to be on the lookout for people trying to smuggle weapons or bomb-making components in their shoes.

—CNN, December 25, 2001

MARCH 4, 2002—September 11 changed everything—at least in the rag trade. "I think there's probably going to be a new sense of humility and a little bit more awareness that fashion doesn't make or break somebody's life," commented a somber John Bartlett, designer of men's wear, explaining his breathtaking decision to display this year's new designs on a mere runway, rather than using his trademark postmodern installations. "I wanted to do something very simple...without all the smoke and mirrors."

The militantly inane world of *haute couture* is unique. In every other aspect of our post-9/11 world, smoke and mirrors still rule.

Airport security remains a farce; between the sleeping security guards, the unplugged machines, and the unlocked doors leading to the tarmac, it's still a lot easier to slip something sharp, pointy or explosive onto a passenger jet in the U.S. than it is in a Third World backwater like the former Soviet republic of Turkmenistan. Entire sectors of the transportation industry—small "general aviation" planes, trucking, buses, passenger and freight trains—don't even use metal detectors, much less subject customers to searches or annoying questions. The Postal Service's primary effort to safeguard the nation's mail is a rule, instituted after the crash of TWA Flight 800, requiring that packages weighing more than sixteen ounces be brought to post offices rather than dropped in boxes. (Heavier packages dropped off in boxes are returned to sender, but not if you insert them in a box in a neighboring Zip code.)

Memo to Osama: Want to mess with the United States? Derail a train full of toxic

DEPARTMENT OF HOMELAND SECURITY PUB. 2002-178

chemicals as it passes through a densely populated area—railroad tracks are rarely fenced in. Set off a few tons of TNT at the base of a busy bridge; any fool with a boat should be able to pull off that trick. Or park a truck bomb on a busy street anywhere in the country; no one will move it unless it's in a no-standing zone.

The future of terrorism, our hapless corporate and political leaders believe, is whatever made headlines last week. Rather than anticipate what might go down in the future, we craft safeguards that only address events that have already happened. The makers of a new $150,000 explosives detector now being marketed to airports claim that their device would have intercepted attempted shoe bomber Richard Reid. Another company, inspired by an incident in which a deranged passenger kicked down a cockpit door, hawks its $18,000 "ThreatDefense" model—if it can stop a nine millimeter bullet, the logic goes, it'll protect you against the drunks in first class.

The trouble is, there won't be any more Richard Reids.

Americans cannot defeat terrorism without addressing its underlying causes: our aggressive, clumsy, bomb-first-ask-questions-later foreign policy; our spectacularly arrogant attitude of cultural and economic expansionism; our unquestioned support of oppressive regimes around the world. Fanatics will always be willing to kill themselves to take on the Great Satan. A kinder and smarter America would deprive those nuts of the widespread financial support they require in order to fund large-scale attacks.

Unless there is a major intellectual breakthrough, however, we Americans are likely to continue the provocations that got us into such trouble in the first place. We'd better learn to live with terrorism—in other words, figure how to minimize the frequency and effectiveness of future attacks. And that means learning to think like terrorists.

What currently passes for airline security, which mainly involves laborious and predictable physical searches, is a sad joke. Hiring thirty thousand more screeners to perform the same task won't help. Islamist extremists and our own homegrown right-wing militia types aren't going to fly more passenger jets into skyscrapers—at least not for the time being. They'll wait until we've forgotten all about 9/11 before attempting a repeat performance.

What would you do if you were in the jihad biz and had limited funding, limited personnel and limited familiarity with your targets? You'd certainly avoid places where security was tight. That's why nothing happened at the Superbowl or Salt Lake City Olympics.

Setting off stolen Russian nukes in lower Manhattan would be theoretically amusing to the Islamists but far too difficult to pull off. In the real world, terrorists choose targets of opportunity and low risk. If you were a politically-minded terrorist determined to destabilize the U.S., you'd leave package bombs in trash cans, mail boxes and train stations. You'd get on a bus, leave your bomb in the luggage rack and get off before the thing blew up. You'd hijack gasoline trucks from truck stops and drive them into the lobbies of government office buildings. You'd strap explosives under your clothing and walk into a crowded mall on the first day of the Christmas shopping season. Or maybe you'd just open fire on a packed sidewalk with a large automatic weapon .

"Sometimes people act as if it's all gone away," Deputy Defense Secretary Paul Wolfowitz said two weeks ago. "I do fear the country has not absorbed that the conflict is far from over." Wolfowitz is one hundred percent correct about the need for vigilance, but his administration's faux war on terror—dispatching troops to prop up corrupt regimes in the Philippines, Yemen and Georgia while stifling dissent here in America—will have little effect beyond causing yet more people to hate us. The key to avoiding another 9/11 is to understand that there won't be any more 9/11s—until there are.

From Little Boy to Big Brother: Bush's Perpetual Warfare

The former commander of NATO forces in Europe fears that America, Britain and their allies could become embroiled in an unwinnable guerrilla war in Afghanistan. General Wesley Clark said in an interview with The Telegraph that there were "worrisome signs" that the allies were drifting into a position similar to that which assailed Soviet forces after their invasion in 1979. "They won big victories to start with," he said. "It took a year or two for the opposition to build up."
—UK Telegraph, March 22, 2002

MARCH 22, 2002—A few years ago, I began working on a graphic-novel update and parody of *1984* a few years ago. An awful lot had changed since George Orwell posited his dystopian vision of the future from his late-1940s deathbed, and I accounted for those differences in my own version, 2001's *2024*. In order to acknowledge the collapse of Soviet Communism and the failure of fascism to reemerge as a potent political force in America, I ditched Orwell's oppressive totalitarian state in favor of an entertainment-fueled nihilism in which dimwitted citizens fritter away their lives watching web TV and working at slightly overpaid jobs to buy worthless junk...on web TV, natch. Where Orwell envisioned endless rows of soldiers marching in perfect unison to the strains of the Two Minute Hate, I saw a world where nations had been replaced by trading blocs and the objects of hatred were the immigrants in our midst.

The six months following The Really Bad Thing That Happened have made clear that I wasn't the only guy boning up on Orwell.

In *1984* the elite Inner Party rules the rattled and irradiated citizens of Oceania through three conduits of fear and intimidation: surveillance, terrorism and perpetual warfare.

The Oceanians had their two-way telescreens; we suffer a ten thousand-employee National Security Agency that relies on automated voice-recognition and keyword software (Echelon, not to be confused with the more picayune and widely reported Carnivore system) to monitor millions of e-mails, faxes and phone calls each day. But few Americans give much thought to this high-tech violation of their privacy; only those who are doing something wrong, they tell themselves, have anything to worry about.

The first eight months of Bush's first term were characterized by political insecurity.

Bush, widely derided as unintelligent and oafish, had carried less than half of the popular vote in 2000, and many Democrats believed that he had bullied his way into the Oval Office. Jim Jeffords' defection from the GOP, partially a reaction to Bush's hard turn to the right after his inauguration, cost Republicans control of the U.S. Senate. Most analysts expected big Democratic gains in the 2002 Congressional elections, due both to the stagnating economy and to historical trends against incumbency in mid-term.

The White House saw 9/11 as a golden opportunity. The first catastrophic terrorist attack on American soil sparked an unprecedented case of leadership projection: desperate for protection and answers (Why do they hate us? Can we kill them before they kill us?), Americans wishfully compared Bush to FDR and Churchill. Approval ratings hit 92 percent. But Bush's political advisors knew that peaking early wouldn't guarantee reelection in 2004. Bush's father had been turned out of office just twenty months after the Gulf War ratcheted his own score up to 91.

The Bushies have lifted their reelection strategy straight out of *1984*, and not just by creating ominous-sounding agencies like the Office of Homeland Security, the supposedly abandoned Office of Strategic Information, and a so-called "Shadow Government." As in *1984*, the Bush regime tolerates zero dissent—a two-party system in name only has been distilled to one in which only Republicans are deemed to express acceptable opinions. Moreover, an absence of follow-up attacks has been met with endless alerts, advisories and empty hysterics in the name of security, most recently culminating with Tom Ridge's rightly-mocked color-code warning system. But Americans don't seem to miss their Democratic Party very much; after all, Clinton spent more time sucking up to big business than worrying about the fact that ordinary people can't afford to see a doctor. And unless Bush resorts

A HOW-TO GUIDE TO REVISIONIST HISTORY

to the Orwellian tactic of setting off bombs to kill his own citizens, the passage of time will inevitably yield to the complacency that could cost him 2004.

That leaves *1984's* most potent political tool: perpetual warfare. Just as Oceania was always at war with Eurasia or Eastasia—who could keep track?—the "war on terror," we are told, will continue indefinitely.

And so hundreds, possibly thousands, of American troops are headed to the Philippines to take on a rag-tag outfit of eighty (!) jungle bandits. Our brave boys in uniform are scouring the back hills of far-flung Yemen in search of al-Qaeda fighters on the lam from our ongoing war in Afghanistan. We've set up new military bases in Uzbekistan, Kyrgyzstan and Tajikistan in order to fight Central Asia's Islamic Movement of Uzbekistan—never mind that the world hasn't heard from them since they kidnapped four American mountain climbers in 2000. China, Indonesia, the former Soviet republic of Georgia, the Axis of Evil, you name it...we're targeting alleged terrorists in anywhere from fifty to sixty countries with tens of thousands of soldiers and tens of billions of dollars. "So long as there's al-Qaeda anywhere, we will help the host countries root them out," Bush says. "If we expect to kill every terrorist in the world, that's going to keep us going beyond doomsday," retorts Senator Robert Byrd.

Best of all for Bush, the more we go after Islamist extremists, the more they'll go after us. The war on terror begets more terror begets more war. That, incredibly, is the point.

The truth is that Bush isn't considering his post-apocalyptic future—at this point November 2004 is all that matters. But by 2004 Cheney or Jeb or some other GOP big-wig will be gearing up for 2008, and after that there'll be a reelection campaign in 2012...old George Orwell, it turns out, wasn't that far off the mark.

The Ugly American Botches a Venezuelan Coup

The Bush administration, which appeared to tacitly endorse the short-lived ouster of Venezuelan President Hugo Chávez, said Tuesday it met in recent months with the opposition there but denied encouraging a coup. But CBS News Senior White House Correspondent John Roberts reports that it appears they did just that by embracing Chávez' successor at a time when U.S. allies in the region were condemning what they clearly saw as a military coup. When Chávez was returned to power, the White House looked like it had sided with coup plotters over democracy. Some Democrats called that deeply troubling.

—CBS News, April 16, 2002

APRIL 16, 2002—You didn't have to blink to miss it. Let the record show that George W. Bush, reconstituted Cold Warrior and ardent defender of democracy, has suffered his first Bay of Pigs. Whether this experience will chasten him as much as it did JFK remains to be seen, but it's still an interesting development.

In a stunning reminder that the Resident's 76 percent approval rating stops at the Rio Grande, an American-backed coup d'état against Venezuela's President Hugo Chávez went from *fait accompli* to farcical footnote in a matter of hours.

It all began at three o'clock in the morning of the 12th of April, when the flamboyantly populist Chávez was arrested by mutinous army officers and unceremoniously replaced by "interim president" Pedro Carmona Estanga. Carmona, chief of a national businessmen's association, immediately reverted to the classic right-wing strongman's playbook. Carmona suspended scheduled elections, tossed out laws regulating big business and promised "a pluralistic vision, democratic, civil and ensuring the implementation of the law." Following that declaration of devotion to democracy, he dissolved both the National Assembly and the Supreme Court.

It comes as little surprise that the Bush Administration, itself the beneficiary of a putsch, would endorse similar subversion elsewhere. But the American media proved astonishingly sanguine at the replacement of a legally elected leader by a 1970s-style junta composed of right-wing army officers and corrupt businessmen. "We know that the Chávez government provoked this crisis," said White House Press Secretary Ari Fleischer in a statement wel-

coming news of the unfolding coup attempt. Describing Carmona as "a respected business leader" in a glowing puff piece, the *New York Times* slammed Chávez as "a ruinous demagogue."

Ruinous, perhaps. Demagogue, maybe. Regardless, Chávez was the legally elected president of Venezuela. What had Chávez done, in the minds of the American establishment, to justify overthrow, exile and the subversion of democracy?

"According to the best information we have, the government suppressed what was a peaceful demonstration of the people," said Fleischer, in reference to an April 11, 2002 incident in which armed men wearing clothes indicating loyalty to Chávez shot thirteen anti-government strikers to death and wounded more than a hundred. It was a tragic incident, but one hardly unique to the Chávez government. Was Fleischer suggesting that the Kent State shootings in 1970 should have precipitated a coup to remove President Richard Nixon?

Chávez's real crime was refusing to suck up to the United States or to its powerful corporate interests. A maverick elected with the overwhelming support of Venezuela's poor in 1998, he routinely referred to his nation's upper classes as "squealing pigs" and "rancid oligarchs." He had a point, too: Venezuela's tiny elite has hogged its immense oil revenues for itself while millions starved.

Unfortunately for the downtrodden masses whose votes propelled Chávez into office, Venezuela produces fifteen percent of America's oil, making the nation of particular economic and geopolitical interest to Washington. In February Chávez, acting on a campaign promise to distribute his country's oil revenues more evenly throughout its impoverished population, replaced Brigadier General Guaicaipuro Lameda as head of the state-owned Petróleos de Venezuela with a politically progressive ally.

Predictably the business community howled in fearful anticipation of further reform. Company officers, fearing that the decades-old systemic corruption that lined their pockets was about to halt, ordered work slowdowns, company-mandated strikes and street demonstrations against their own government in the hope of crippling the economy and destabilizing Chávez's rule.

The *Times'* hit piece summed up the case against Chávez succinctly: "He courted Fidel Castro and Saddam Hussein, battled the media and alienated virtually every constituency from middle-class professionals, academics and business leaders to union members and the Roman Catholic Church." He visited nations despised by the U.S., including Libya and Iran, and criticized the "war on terror." And he dedicated his rule to forcing business to share profits with ordinary citizens. In short, Chávez remained loyal to his leftist principles and to the desperately poor constituency who had elected him.

But to the Bushies it didn't matter whether or not the Venezuelan people liked him or approved of him. They saw democracy as inconvenient. Chávez had to go.

It's too soon to know for certain whether the CIA tried to engineer an Allende-style operation in Venezuela, but anyone who's read ex-spy Philip Agee's seminal CIA exposé *Inside the Company* recognizes classic signs emanating from New York and Washington: official statements of encouragement are laced with just enough ambiguity to provide plausible deniability; blithe dismissals of democratic principles in friendly media are followed by rapid reversals if and when things start to go wrong. Don't be too surprised if those gun-toting "Chávez supporters" who opened fire on April 11 ultimately turn out to be CIA-employed provocateurs.

But wait, it gets better: Chávez, while held captive on the Venezuelan Caribbean island of La Orchila the weekend of the attempted coup, noticed an American jet on the runway, and presumed it was waiting to take him into exile. "I saw the plane. It bore the markings of a private plane from the United States, not an official plane...What was it doing there?" Chávez asked, noting that the American ambassador to Venezuela clearly recognized the plane.

Days passed without a Bush Administration denial of involvement in the coup. Finally, on April 16, Ari Fleischer acknowledged that State Department Assistant Secretary for Western Hemisphere Affairs Otto J. Reich had telephoned coup leader Carmona hours after Chávez's ouster. In that call, according to Fleischer, Reich asked Carmona not to dismiss the National Assembly in order to avoid offending world opinion.

Operation Caracas went wrong nearly the second it started. Even a fervent U.S. ally, Mexican President Vincente Fox, joined Fidel Castro in condemning the coup and refusing to recognize the new regime. Soon every government in the Western hemisphere except our own had condemned the coup. Tens of thousands of Venezuelan demonstrators took to the streets demanding Chávez's return. By April 13, Carmona had replaced Chávez in the pokey and the U.S. State Department was calling for the "return of democracy."

Asked whether the U.S. knew about the coup in advance, Fleischer waffled. True, numerous anti-Chávez activists had visited the White House in recent weeks to request U.S. help in deposing the president, but the White House refused to admit that they had encouraged the plotters. "We explicitly told opposition leaders that the United States would not support a coup," he said. He wouldn't say, however, whether the U.S. ultimately green-lighted a covert action.

"I haven't said that this conspiracy [against me] has its roots in the United States," President Chávez said April 15. He didn't need to.

Bush Turns Assassin

In the U.S. view, Gulbuddin Hekmatyar is a villain who deserves a violent death, although he is different from the al-Qaeda and Taliban leaders previously targeted by the military and CIA in Afghanistan. The CIA took a shot at Hekmatyar with a missile from one of its unmanned Predator drones on Monday near Kabul, but missed, defense officials said. The missile killed some of his followers. U.S. officials accuse Hekmatyar of plotting attacks on American troops, offering rewards for their deaths and trying to destabilize the U.S.-backed interim government of Hamid Karzai. At the same time, officials acknowledge that Hekmatyar, who once served as Afghanistan's prime minister, has limited ties to the Taliban and is only suspected of working with al-Qaeda. But they say his anti-U.S. activities make him a more immediate threat than the other feuding warlords.

—Associated Press, May 10, 2002

MAY 14, 2002—This is fair to say: Gulbuddin Hekmatyar, a 55-year-old Pashtun warlord, is a bad man. Evil, possibly. "What we're talking about here is someone at the absolute margin of violence in Afghan society—in his own way someone as extreme as Osama bin Laden," Anthony Cordesman, a defense analyst at the Center for Strategic and International Studies, said in an interview. "He has a history that has proved about as conclusively as anyone can that this is a violent, vicious man who deserves to be a target."

A target of what? A target of whom? Hang tight through the next 124 words:

While his Hezb-e-Islami faction was part of a coalition fighting the Soviet army during the 1980s, Hekmatyar earned a reputation for treachery and over-the-top violence that shocked even war-hardened Afghan sensibilities. His militia, say more moderate warlords, killed more innocent Afghans than Soviets. Notches on his gun include the murders of at least two BBC journalists and Dr. Sayed Burhannudin Madjruh, an Afghan intellectual who was one of his nation's leading poets. As prime minister for the Northern Alliance government, Hekmatyar ruled the city of Kabul for a few months during 1996 before being ousted by Taliban troops; in an effort to out-Taliban the Taliban, he banned movies, music and soccer. He was financed in his exploits by both the CIA and Pakistani intelligence.

None of this, however, explains why the CIA tried to assassinate him on May 6.

"We had information," an anonymous Pentagon official told the *New York Times*'

Thomas Shanker, "that he was planning attacks on American and coalition forces, on the interim government and on [interim president Hamid] Karzai himself."

You and I, faced with such "information," might have had Hekmatyar picked up for questioning. We might put him and his pals on trial for conspiracy and, if he were found guilty, throw him in prison. But the guys in the White House aren't like us. They're gangsters. Gangsters are above the law. Gangsters don't bother with judges and juries. They pay off judges; they have their enemies whacked.

And so your illegitimate gangster government, less than a month after it attempted to overthrow the democratically elected government of Venezuela, sent one of those unmanned Predator drone planes into the blue skies over the Hindu Kush. Some dude punched a button on an iMac at an undisclosed location in the Virginia suburbs and fired a Hellfire missile at Hekmatyar's car convoy on a road just outside Kabul. "I believe some others were killed in the strike, but the target escaped," an unnamed U.S. official told Reuters.

Just when the Bush Administration seems to have achieved its ultimate blend of hubris, stupidity and viciousness, it outdoes itself. First the U.S. government, despite repeatedly being suckered by Afghan factions into attacking their rivals, chooses to believe Karzai's accusations of a Hekmatyar plot. Then, rather than letting the Afghans sort out their internal politics for themselves—in Afghanistan, warlords *are* the politicians—the Bushies decide to murder the dude.

"While foreign troops are present, the interim government does not have any value or meaning," Hekmatyar declared in a February statement calling for the U.S. to leave Afghanistan. Don't be surprised, now that we've tried to kill him, if Hekmatyar really does go after Americans. Naturally, the Bushies' perverse logic would view that as vindication.

WARS OF THE FUTURE WILL FOLLOW A POLICY OF *RETROACTIVE PREEMPTION*: THE EXCUSE FOR WAR WILL BE DETERMINED AS THE *RESULT* OF FIGHTING IT.

SINCE ALMOST EVERY COUNTRY IS GUILTY OF *SOMETHING*, VIRTUALLY ANY INVASION CAN BE JUSTIFIED AFTER THE FACT.

EVEN IN THE CASE OF WARS AGAINST NATIONS THAT TURN OUT TO HAVE BEEN INNOCENT, THE POST FACTO DOCTRINE STILL APPLIES.

BEST OF ALL, AGGRESSORS CAN PREVENT GETTING ATTACKED THEMSELVES BY APPLYING THE COROLLARY OF ANTICIPATORY PACIFISM.

"The attack on Mr. Hekmatyar...was the first confirmed mission to kill a factional leader who was not officially part of the fallen Taliban government or al-Qaeda terrorist network," the *Times* wrote on May 9. In fact, Hekmatyar was militantly anti-Taliban and anti-al-Qaeda. He was targeted because he opposes the U.S. occupation and his support for America's hand-picked Afghan leader, Hamid Karzai, has been less than wholehearted.

Ironically, Hekmatyar's Afghan street cred is infinitely broader than Karzai's. Karzai has no militia and no experience fighting the Soviets. He spent the late 1990s as a Unocal oil employee sucking up to the Taliban in the hopes that they'd allow his company to run a pipeline through the territory they held. Were the U.S. to pull out today, Karzai would be out of power tomorrow. Hekmatyar, on the other hand, is an influential member of the party in power, out of favor with the current president but respected by a substantial portion of the population.

But that's not the point. The point is this: Article 2 of the United Nations Charter, as well as the U.S. Army's field manual, prohibits "assassination, proscription, or outlawry of an enemy, or putting a price upon an enemy's head, as well as offering a reward for an enemy 'dead or alive.'" Beginning in 1976, after the CIA was implicated in the death of Chilean President Salvadore Allende and at least eight attempts on Fidel Castro, Presidents Ford, Carter and Reagan each issued executive orders banning U.S. agencies from commiting political assassinations. Reagan's Executive Order 12333 states that "no person employed by or acting on behalf of the United States Government shall engage in, or conspire to engage in, assassination." That executive order, confirmed by Bush Sr., Clinton and Bush Jr., remains in force.

Bush broke that law. Hekmatyar is a bad guy, but so is Bush. He should resign and face prosecution for attempted murder.

Liars, Morons or Both?

I'm proud of what this group of Americans have done on the football field. No more proud than those who wear the blue, I might add. And I'm proud of your commitment to our country. See, this enemy of ours, they don't understand the Air Force Academy or what it stands for. They thought we were weak—of course, they never saw the Air Force football team play. They thought we'd just roll over. They thought we might file a couple of lawsuits. They found out we think differently here in America.
—George W. Bush, May 17, 2002

MAY 21, 2002—It only lasted a few seconds, but on May 17, George W. Bush had a Bill Clinton moment, and it was magical. "Had I known that the enemy was going to use airplanes to kill on that fateful morning," George W. Bush reassured us, "I would have done everything in my power to protect the American people." Did he realize how much he sounded like his prevaricating predecessor? Were the subject something other than the murder of three thousand innocent people, Bush's desperate dissembling would be absolutely hilarious.

In the circus of hypocrites that is the Bush Administration, the best lines are reserved for the ringmaster. On that same day Dick Cheney warned Democrats not to "seek political advantage by making incendiary suggestions...that the White House had advance information that would have prevented the tragic events of 9/11. Such commentary," he emphasized, "is thoroughly irresponsible and totally unworthy of national leaders in a time of war."

First: what war? Congress hasn't declared war since 1941. And when it comes to "political advantage," it's the Bushies, not the Democrats, who have taken advantage of 9/11 to further their partisan political agenda. They used the dead of New York, Pennsylvania and Washington to push for such non-terror-related Republican platform planks as "fast track" signing authority on free trade agreements, Internet censorship, tax cuts for the rich and drilling for oil in the Arctic National Wildlife Refuge. To be sure, there's a war going on: a PR war. And now that Democrats are finally scoring a few points of their own, Bushies who have been slam-dunking for months are screaming foul.

"Bush Knew," the *New York Post* screamed last week. Did he? Hell if I know. Here's a man who subverted constitutional law in order to seize the White House in a judicial coup d'état, who claimed while campaigning to be a "compassionate conservative" but revealed himself to be a Genghis Khan right-winger as soon as he took office, and who told us up

front after 9/11 that his administration would routinely lie for the sake of the "war on terror." Under normal circumstances, the mere suggestion that a president would deliberately stand idly by as his citizens were slaughtered en masse would be appalling. George W. Bush, however, tells Congress to go to hell whenever it requests documents or summons his staff to testify at hearings. Such a man, it's difficult to avoid concluding, is capable of anything.

There's no smoking gun—evidence that Bush was told in advance about the specifics of 9/11—so far. But it's hard to escape an inevitable, disturbing conclusion that itself bears consideration: We are in the hands of liars, morons or both.

When Terrormemogate first hit the airwaves, the administration trotted out National Security Advisor Condoleezza Rice, who also serves as chief of Bush's Counterterrorism Security Group, to face the cameras. Rice repeatedly asserted that pre-9/11 threats of airplane hijackings by Islamist terrorists had been so vague as to be useless. This is somewhat believable: any firefighter can tell you that false alarms outnumber real fires. Now, let's say you're the President of the United States. You're told that someone (you don't know who) may hijack passenger jets (you don't know when, how or how many). You assume, as Rice says the Bushies did, that those hijackings will assume a traditional historical model: demands for money and/or release of prisoners in exchange for the release of hostages. What do you do?

Given such a generalized threat, you'd undoubtedly order your Air Force to a state of high alert. Even "traditional" hijackings, after all, tend to end badly, with innocent passengers getting shot full of holes. You'd keep planes in the air and many more on the ground, ready to scramble at a second's notice in case the terrorists strike. If months went by without any hijackings, you might decide to lower the nation's state of readiness.

On the morning of September 11, 2001, though, only eight fighters were assigned to defend the United States of America's 3,618,770-square-mile airspace. These eight planes were piloted by weekend warriors, members of the Air National Guard. And our jets weren't even in the air; they were sitting on the ground at the time of the attacks. America's state of readiness, despite the huge military defense budget that sucks millions away from starving children, compared unfavorably to Thailand's when disaster struck.

By Rice's own admission, the Bush Administration ignored the vague, imprecise threats of which Bush was informed during his month-long August vacation, simply because the intelligence reports didn't specify exact times and dates.

"Administration officials insisted all last week that turning a plane into a suicide bomb was something that nobody had contemplated," *Time* magazine reports in its May 27 issue. "But that just isn't so. In 1995, authorities in the Philippines scuppered a plan—masterminded by Razmi Yousef, who had also plotted the 1993 World Trade Center bombing—for mass hijackings of American planes over the Pacific. Evidence developed during the investigation of Yousef and his partner, Abdul Hakim Murad, uncovered a plan to crash a plane into CIA headquarters in Langley, Virginia. And as long ago as 1994, in an incident that is well known among terrorism experts, French authorities foiled a plot by the Algerian Armed Islamic Group to fly an airliner into the Eiffel Tower."

No matter how you look at it, Condi Rice was either clueless or lying. Everybody knew that Islamist jihadis had plotted suicide hijackings well before 9/11. Nevertheless, the Bushies did nothing to improve airline security. They did nothing to prepare for the possibility of hijackings, whether suicide or traditional. They didn't even tell the airlines what they knew. Then, after 9/11, they covered up the fact that they had received numerous warnings.

Moron Bush or Liar Bush—I don't care which one answers the White House phone. Would one of you please resign?

George W. Kafka

President Bush said Tuesday a "full-scale manhunt" was under way for al-Qaeda operatives following the capture of suspected terrorist Jose Padilla. "We will run down every lead, every hint," Mr. Bush told reporters at the White House. Padilla, a 33-year-old U.S. citizen also known as Abdullah al Muhajir, was detained by the FBI in Chicago on May 8, when he arrived from Pakistan. He was held without charge until being declared an "enemy combatant" on Sunday, after which he was transferred to a naval brig in South Carolina, officials said. Military officials have not decided whether to charge him or what charges to file, said Pentagon spokesman Lt. Col. Rivers Johnson. "Padilla's where he needs to be," Mr. Bush said. Attorney General John Ashcroft and other U.S. officials said Padilla was allegedly plotting to detonate a radioactive "dirty" bomb in the U.S., probably in Washington D.C. But some U.S. officials now admit they're not sure what Padilla's plans were when he returned to the U.S. last month.
—Associated Press, June 11, 2002

JUNE 11, 2002—It can happen to you.

The jackbooted thugs can arrest you without bothering to accuse you of a crime. They can deprive you of the right to make a phone call, to receive a visit from your family, or even to see a lawyer. It doesn't matter if you're innocent or not; our state-sanctioned terrorists can keep you locked up in prison for the rest of your life without ever granting you your day in court.

But you're an American citizen, you protest. It makes no difference whatsoever: you still have no rights.

After cynically using the 9/11 attacks as a pretext to eradicate one civil liberty after another, the Bush Administration has finally stripped away the single most essential freedom of an American citizen: the right to due process before a jury of his peers. Classifying 33-year-old Chicagoan Jose Padilla as an al-Qaeda associate and "enemy combatant," Attorney General John Ashcroft authorized his transfer from a federal courthouse in New York City, where he had been held as a "material witness" on a customs violation since May 8, to indefinite military detention at the Charleston Naval Weapons Station in South Carolina.

Though not legally charged, Padilla, who changed his name to Abdullah al-Mujahir after converting to Islam, is accused of planning to build and detonate a non-nuclear "dirty" radioactive bomb, possibly in Washington, D.C. Government officials concede that they have no physical evidence against Padilla—bomb components, manuals, etc. Their case, they admit, relies primarily on information from star canary Abu Zubaydah, a captured al-Qaeda operative whose Guantánamo debriefing sparked last month's flurry of warnings from Homeland Security czar Tom Ridge. Justice Department officials, an anonymous official told the *New York Times* on June 12, "concluded that they could not bring a winnable court prosecution, largely because the evidence against [Padilla] was derived from intelligence sources and other witnesses the government cannot or will not produce in court."

So much for the right to face your accuser.

Padilla theoretically faces prosecution under a military tribunal. (Back in November, you may remember, Bush had promised that tribunals would only be used against foreigners. Changing times require flexible thinking.) But Defense Secretary Donald Rumsfeld says that even kangaroo court justice is probably a long way off: "We're not interested in trying him at this moment." Some officials say that detainees like Padilla and those being held in the Guantánamo dog kennel need not be tried until the end of the "war on terror"—which, according to Bush himself, could go on forever.

America may well be a safer place because Jose Padilla has been "disappeared," in the brutal lexicon of Latin American death squads. But the manner in which this American has been deprived of his citizenship rights—to a lawyer, to a speedy trial, to apply for bail—is reminiscent of such totalitarian states as Nazi Germany and the Soviet Union. What the Bushies are doing to Padilla is an outrage—and it could happen to any of us.

The legal basis for this action is a twisted farce. "Citizens who associate themselves with the military arm of the enemy government, and with its aid, guidance and direction enter this country bent on hostile acts, are enemy belligerents," ruled the Supreme Court in a precedent-setting case in 1942, during World War II. The United States, however, is not at war. Congress has not declared war against the Taliban or anyone else. And while Padilla may indeed have plotted hostile acts at the behest of al-Qaeda, no one accuses him of belonging to the Taliban army. How could they? The Bushies denied P.O.W. status under the Geneva Convention to Guantánamo inmates by arguing that the Taliban never had an army.

The war on terror, like the war on drugs, isn't a state of combat. It's an advertising slogan. The bombing campaign against Afghanistan is, at most, a police action. And while there are undoubtedly organizations like al-Qaeda that hate the U.S. foreign policy and mean harm to Americans, there is no legal basis for denaturalizing Americans merely because they're accused of belonging to such groups. You wouldn't know it by listening to Bush & Co., but there's no law, by the way, against hating the U.S.

Ironically, this vile assault on essential American rights comes on the heels of what seems to be a previous Bush Administration abuse of Padilla's rights—he was jailed in New York for a month without being charged with a crime. Ruling in a different case, New York federal judge Shira Scheindlin wrote recently that "relying on the material witness statute to detain people who are presumed innocent under our Constitution in order to prevent potential crimes is an illegitimate use of the statute." That ruling may have inspired Padilla's transfer to the South Carolina military lock-up.

You're probably not all that troubled about what happened to Padilla. You haven't hung out with Islamic extremists, boned up on your bomb-making skills or fantasized about Chernobylizing the Washington Mall. But don't forget: a court of law still hasn't proved that Jose Padilla did either. And if George W. Bush gets his way, it never will.

It's the Economy Again

President Bush said on Monday the U.S. economy was suffering from a hangover after a 1990s "economic binge" but was fundamentally strong despite the slide in stocks to nearly five-year lows. Bush offered an upbeat assessment of the economy, pointing to low inflation and interest rates, "sound" monetary policy, rising productivity, and relatively strong retail sales as he sought to soothe investors made uneasy by accounting scandals at firms like Enron Corp. and WorldCom Inc.

The Dow Jones industrial average, down nearly 250 points before Bush's remarks, weakened as he spoke...By early afternoon it was off 351 points, or 4 percent, at 8,333.

—Arshad Mohammed, Reuters, July 15, 2002

JULY 16, 2002—Like his father, George W. Bush just doesn't get it.

"I want you to know that our economy is fundamentally strong, this economy has got the foundations for growth," Bush said July 15. "This economy is coming back, that's the fact." Yet unemployment continues to increase faster than expected, the federal budget deficit is skyrocketing and stocks are at their lowest levels since 1997. More businesses are going bankrupt than are being launched and debt delinquencies are at a ten-year high. Interest rates and inflation remain low, but there isn't enough investment capital or discretionary consumer income for that good news to begin generating jobs—and jobs are the single greatest indicator and predictor of recovery.

Recovery? Hell—we're in the middle of a big ol' fat recession. And since W., like his dad, can't seem to locate the vision thing, there's no end in sight.

To be fair, Bush inherited much of this mess. Not only did the dot-com crash throw hundreds of thousands of people out of work, but President Clinton failed to invest the proceeds of the boom in federal programs—education, socialized medicine, extended jobless benefits, infrastructure projects—that might have helped us weather the inevitable bust. The positive side of that impecuniousness was a legacy of fiscal discipline—a wet dream come true for GOP budget hawks. Clinton's last budget, for 2001, left a $135 billion surplus. Analysts had predicted a $5 trillion surplus over the next decade—enough to repay the entire accumulated deficit.

On July 12, Bush's Office of Management and Budget announced, Enron-like, that all of America's money had vanished. A $1.35 trillion tax cut for the extravagantly rich, huge

89

payoffs to well-connected defense contractors and appropriations for the Department of Homeland Security and Curtailed Individual Rights have gobbled up more than $4 trillion. Bush will succeed Ronald Reagan as the biggest tax-and-spend president in history.

But we can't afford his money-wasting ways.

If things were as bad now as they're going to get, we could tough it out—and so could Bush. But as more people take up positions on the dole queue, his mile-wide-inch-deep popularity will continue to evaporate. Future Democratic administrations will have to—as they usually do after GOP recessions—dig the country out of the debt run up by fiscal "conservatives."

The trouble is that the accounting scandal that brought down Enron, WorldCom and Xerox is far graver than a short-term cyclical correction. It threatens to undermine the foundation of market-based capitalism itself. Bush addressed investors twice in one week, but his patently false assurances that help is on the way only drove jittery securities exchanges to record lows. "For lack of a better description, you have as much full-fledged panic as you are going to get," commented Tony Cecin, director of institutional trading at U.S. Bancorp Piper Jaffray in Minneapolis. "The negative mentality is as pervasive as I have ever seen it, and I went through [the] '73 and '74 bear market."

The panic is real and it is rational: Investors finally realize that they can't trust earnings and other "audited" figures released by corporations. Absent that information, they can't evaluate stocks, which leads to only one logical conclusion: sell everything and stay out of the market. "Independent accounting" was BS all along; even companies that didn't bribe their auditing firms outright with lucrative consulting deals controlled them via the millions of dollars in fees paid out for their signing off on company financial statements. It's hardly a unique moment in history to discover that some shepherds have been munching on lampchops from a flock they swore to protect. But even the most scrupulously honest auditors rely on *their clients* for the numbers they crunch. Unless corporations grant auditors full subpoena powers, they remain the sole source for the figures used to assess their own financial health.

Reagan-era deregulation is the real culprit here. Executives were less inclined to outright fraud during the 1980s, when the liberal-run Securities and Exchange Commission loved to jail insider traders like Ivan Boesky. Financial irregularities were widespread even then, but on a smaller scale. The current Arthur Andersen meltdown became inevitable when the aftermath of the post-regulation '90s collided with the dot-commers' unique proclivities for fictional bookkeeping.

It's hard to envision a solution that doesn't rely on heavy-handed government intervention. Perhaps companies could be taxed on their gross revenues, the proceeds going into a federal fund to be used to hire independent auditors, the same way the Defense Department hires private contractors. Alternatively, the IRS could be expanded to handle the additional regulatory burden. Even so, government auditors would necessarily rely on numbers provided by the businesses themselves. Auditing, like taxation, ultimately runs on the honor system.

Disgruntled employees could be offered cash rewards for turning in their bosses for book-cooking, but even trolling for whistle-blowers wouldn't guarantee corporate transparency. Everyone agrees that Bush's proposed remedies—doubling jail terms for wire fraud from five to ten years, hiring more SEC investigators—are meaningless.

"He certainly is addressing a problem that needs to be addressed—the serial failure of any of these corporations to act in a manner consistent with their obligations to shareholders and employees—but I wonder whether any of these proposals indeed have teeth in

them," replied Gerard Treanor, a Washington lawyer who defends white-collar executives. "A lot of this is same-old, same-old," added Brian Hoffmann, a corporate lawyer in New York. "People are going to see this for what it is, which is a political response."

Which is why the markets are sliding.

Bush claims that the economy will improve if Congress grants him fast-track negotiating authority on free trade and makes his $1.5 trillion tax cut permanent beyond ten years. These claims are absurd on their face: President Clinton never obtained fast track but nevertheless presided over the biggest economic boom in U.S. history. (His free-trade agreements, however, caused joblessness to go up and average wages to fall.) And even if you buy Bush's discredited retro-Reagan trickle-down scheme—tax the poor and middle class, hand the cash to the rich so they can spend it, creating jobs for the poor and middle class—no one thinks those results will begin to show before the 2004 election. The unemployed need jobs *now*, not in 2012.

There are two main problems facing the U.S. economy: the accounting fiasco and the dot-com crash. On the latter, Bush should acknowledge that his economic policy has been a mistake. He should call for an immediate repeal of his ill-advised tax giveaway, cancel the "war on terror" military boondoggle and signal a return to the fiscal discipline of the Clinton years. He has a good cover story—times are simply tougher than we thought they'd be. Today's investors love nothing more than a realistic deficit hawk.

Accounting fraud is closely tied to CEO greed. Corporate executives skim obscene salaries off the top of revenues, getting paid tens of millions of dollars while driving venerable companies out of business and hard-working employees out of work. Companies argue that these payouts are necessary to find and retain the very best managers, but history disproves that canard: Plenty of talented executives work for significantly less, and plenty of overpaid greedheads do a lousy job. CEO pay ought to be capped, as the Securities and Exchange Commission proposed a decade ago, at twenty times the income of the lowest-paid employee. Such a measure would insure that all boats are lifted by a rising tide and protect shareholders from rapacious executives.

The Coca-Cola corporation recently announced that it will begin treating stock options as an expense on its balance sheet, but that fix doesn't go far enough. Giving free options and stocks to CEOs encourages decisions designed to increase short-term profitability at the expense of a company's long-term wellbeing. (Creative accounting temporarily increases a company's stock price, encouraging executive CEOs to "pump and dump" their shares.) CEOs should be hired and fired like any other employee; their salaries should be flat paychecks with raises tied to inflation and performance. To truly prevent insider double-dealing, CEOs must be banned from owning shares of their own or related corporations.

Finally, while longer jail terms for corporate criminals won't have much impact on boardroom behavior, it makes moral sense to hold those who steal millions as responsible for their crimes as those who steal hundreds. For instance, it's high time the SEC took a serious look at George W. Bush's $848,560 windfall when he was director of Texas' Harken Energy Corp. in 1991. Bush dumped the stock at four dollars a share, weeks before Harken announced a large quarterly loss. By the time he reported the sale (eight months late), it was worth a buck a share to ordinary investors without inside knowledge of the company's financials. Strangely, SEC Chairman Harvey Pitt refuses to release his agency's documents on the subject. "Unless there's a reason to re-open ancient history, we should move on," he said on July 14.

I can think of 848,560 good reasons.

George and Adolf's Permanent Revolution

A reported remark by a German minister comparing President Bush's tactics over Iraq to those of Hitler envenomed a close-fought German election today and demonstrated how anti-Americanism had moved to the center of political debate here.
—New York Times, September 20, 2002

OCTOBER 2, 2002—Herta Daeubler-Gmelin got it half-right when she compared George W. Bush's tactics to Adolf Hitler's. "Bush wants to divert attention from his domestic problems," she told *Schwaebisches Tagblatt* on September 18. "It's a classic tactic. It's one that Hitler also used."

Shortly after Ms. Daeubler-Gmelin made her remarks, Bush flung his long knives across the Atlantic, and within days she was no longer Germany's justice minister.

Such sovereignty-busting gangsterism has its pleasures, but Bush's biggest cribbing from the Hitler playbook is "permanent revolution." Developed by socialist theorist Leon Trotsky in 1915 and perverted in its application by such totalitarian masters of control as Hitler, Stalin and Mao Tse-Tung, permanent revolution is the pinnacle of the art of mass distraction—one continually changes the subject of debate by striving for new goals that are always just beyond reach. The concept is diabolically simple: by the time people start grumbling about the problems created by your Great Leap Forward, you're causing new difficulties with your Cultural Revolution. Opposition takes time to materialize; taking the nation from one crisis to the next neutralizes your enemies by focusing their efforts against initiatives you've already abandoned.

On the domestic front, Bush has launched so many political offensives that it's impossible for what's left of the left to launch a coordinated resistance. Expanding free trade, another round of tax cuts for the wealthy and corporations while running up the deficit, trashing the environment, rounding up detainees and depriving them of due process, union-busting, curtailing privacy rights—any one of these full-scale assaults would require a full-court press by liberals to block or overturn.

Virtually everything on the right-wing wish list is now being proposed in the current blizzard of legislative and regulatory activity. Previous presidents spaced out their initiatives in order to build popular support; Bush prefers to leave elected representatives out of the equation. The more legislation he throws at the wall, the more he'll get passed—and the

more people will forget that his is an illegal regime.

Generalissimo El Busho's policy of permanent revolution reached its zenith with his post-September 11 foreign policy. Before we allow Bush's razzle-dazzle to leap us ahead to his next war, let's consider the one we've already got. Our campaign in Afghanistan, lest we forget, continues even as thousands more troops pack for Iraq.

"Dead or alive," growled George W. Bush, squinting hard at Osama bin Laden and Mullah Omar. If we couldn't get those two, he said, we'd settle for any other high-ranking al-Qaeda or Taliban official we could find. A year later our highest-profile prisoner is alleged al-Qaeda senior field commander Abu Zubaydah. Zubaydah was not involved, says the U.S., in any of the major attacks—9/11, our East African embassies, the *U.S.S. Cole*—but rather in two Y2K plots that never came off (blowing up LAX and a tourist hotel in Jordan). Hardly a big fish, he's just a little minnow—and we wouldn't even have him if the Pakistanis hadn't toooed him into our boat.

We blew it. U.S. taxpayers are spending between $500 million and $1 billion a month to occupy Afghanistan and fight its Islamiot guerrillas (in the 1980s we called them "freedom fighters"), yet we haven't caught any of the people we blame for 9/11. Al-Qaeda remains operational. They're moving money, weapons and men around the Middle East and Central Asia, preparing for their next attack. Not only are you no safer than you were on September 10, 2001, you've spent billions of bucks along the way.

But wait a minute, Bush said, beginning to distance himself from Operation Enduring Failure: the Afghan war was never about finding Osama and his coconspirators. No, he revises, we actually went to Afghanistan to liberate its people.

"We've seen the pictures of joy when we liberated city after city in Afghanistan," Bush

crowed on December 12. "And none of us will ever forget the laughter and the music and the cheering and the clapping at a stadium that was once used for public execution. Children now fly kites and they play games. Women now come out of their homes from house arrest, able to walk the streets without chaperons."

Beautiful imagery, nicely written by a talented but sadly anonymous White House speechwriter and echoed by TV reports filed from the Kabul Intercontinental Hotel. Too bad that, except for the part about games and kites, it's a lie.

Public executions continue. Sharia law—stoning adulterers and chopping off the arms of thieves—remains in effect, enforced by the same judges who ruled under the Taliban. Aside from a tiny minority of the residents of Kabul, ruled by Hamid Karzai's U.S.-protected city-state, the "liberated" women of Afghanistan still wear the *burqa*. A May report issued by Human Rights Watch says that women are subjected to "sexual violence by armed factions and public harassment" and that gang rapes are commonplace, particularly in the northern part of the country. Not one inch of road has been paved. Writing for the *Lexington Herald-Tribune*, Sudarsan Raghavan notes: "The fall of the Taliban has left a power vacuum in mostly ethnic-Pashtun southern Afghanistan that has been filled by scores of *shuras*, from provincial ones to others in small villages. Elsewhere, warlords such as Abdul Rashid Dostum in the northern city of Mazar-e-Sharif and Ismael Khan in the western province of Herat are now firmly in control of their fiefdoms, just as they were before the Taliban emerged in 1994. Along one stretch, the road is dotted with armed men at checkpoints controlled by tribal *shuras*. Often, they are nothing more than highway robbers preying on commercial trucks and taxis."

What about all the money that we promised to spend to rebuild the country we bombed

into freedom? Surprise: the West welshed. The Karzai government is already so broke that it can't pay its employees; it's already running a budget deficit—$165 million by early next year. Two billion dollars has already been spent—much of it likely stolen by corrupt Afghan officials—while the lives of ordinary Afghans continue to be plagued by poverty and starvation.

It doesn't take an expert on Central Asian politics to discern the obvious: occupation by a rich country that makes poor people even poorer is a recipe for resentment. Afghans are among the world's most fiercely independent people. A self-indulgent Western superpower propping up a band of third-rate puppets isn't helping to reduce anti-Americanism there. Never doubt that similar sentiments are commonplace throughout other Muslim countries.

One might ask why our Generalissimo is going after Saddam Hussein's Iraq while the war in Afghanistan has worked out so poorly, but one would be missing the point: Trotsky's theory of permanent revolution is at work. It is precisely *because* we botched Afghanistan that we're moving on to Iraq.

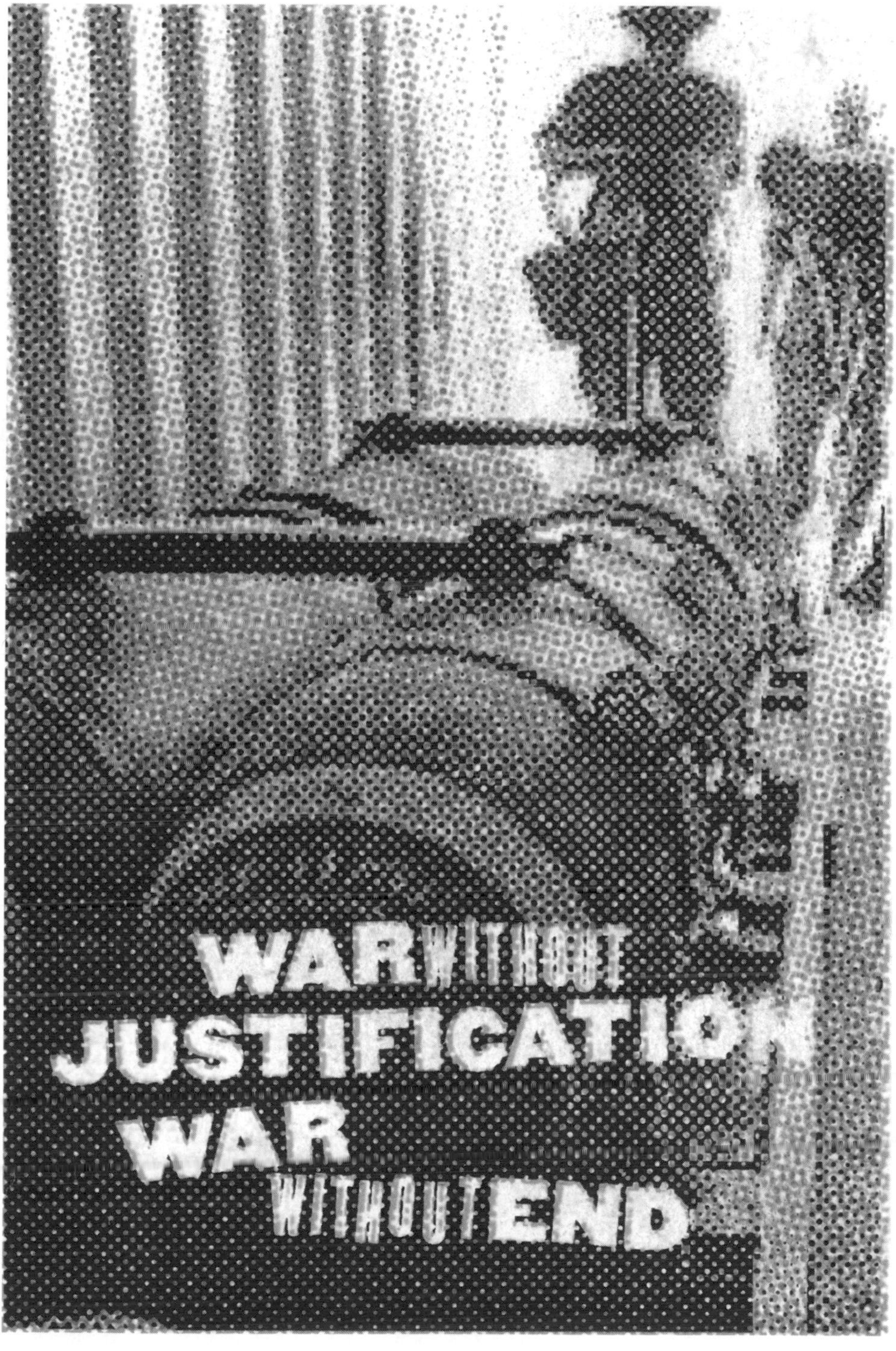
WAR WITHOUT
JUSTIFICATION
WAR
WITHOUT END

The Empire Strikes Back Again, Redux, Part 2

Saddam Hussein is producing deadly plague viruses in an under-ground laboratory beneath a hospital, evidence put before a Congressional hearing indicated yesterday. Richard Butler, the for-mer head of the United Nations weapons inspections team in Iraq, said recent signs that the Iraqi President was manufacturing the plague and the highly contagious Ebola virus were "very credible." He also said that Iraq was close to developing a nuclear capability. Khidir Hamza, a former Iraqi nuclear engineer who defected in 1994, said that Saddam was within three years of equipping three nuclear weapons with bomb-grade uranium. Iraq has more than ten tons of uranium and one ton of slightly enriched uranium, he said, quoting German intelligence.

— Times of London, August 1, 2002

AUGUST 1, 2002 — Should we send in 250,000 ground troops or will 25,000-pound bombs be enough? Do they have nerve gas, and if so would they use it? What about the Republican Guards — are they as fierce, smart and loyal as advertised?

How many people will die?

It's the middle of a Bush administration, so it must be time to distract a recession-bat-tered public with saber-rattling tirades equating Iraqi leader Saddam Hussein with Adolf Hitler. How else can Bush get his approval rating back up from 65 to 92 percent? But sell-ing Americans on *Gulf War Boondoggle 2: The Revenge* will likely prove more difficult than convincing them to show up for the 1991 original. As Congressmen Chuck Hagel (R-NE) points out, "There are a number of difficult questions that need to be asked before Congress would support a resolution of war against Iraq."

First, there's no inciting incident: Saddam hasn't invaded Kuwait. The guy is making no effort to dis us properly! Second, the highly anticipated ending of the first *Gulf War*, in which columns of victorious American troops were to be showered with roses and free oil by liber-ated Iraqis, never materialized. Third, the Afghan action epic *Tora Bora Bora*, though ini-tially well received, is now considered trite, clichéd and banal. Fourth, this expensive sequel would probably be financed exclusively by the United States. A July 27, *London Times* poll shows that most Britons, our biggest partners in the original *GWB*, are not interested in

watching a sequel.

The rationale for attacking Iraq changes by the day, according to administration insiders. First came the unfinished-business argument: Saddam invaded Kuwait in 1990, used chemical gas and remains a threat in the Middle East. Never mind that the Iraqi dictator worked for our CIA when he did that stuff, and that nothing worse has transpired in Iraq during the last twelve years than garden-variety Third World repression. Then Bush declared Iraq a member of an "Axis of Evil" along with Iran and North Korea, unrelated countries that share neither common ideological nor geopolitical aims. Finally, Defense Secretary Donald Rumsfeld implied a link between Iraq and al-Qaeda in planning the September 11, 2001 attacks. Rummy says "absolute proof" isn't necessary to justify an invasion. That merely confirms that we don't have any.

"[The Bushies] don't seem to have a cohesive message to describe the threat," a U.S. government analyst commented to Reuters' Carol Giacomo. "They seem to be throwing things at the wall to see what might stick and nothing's taking hold."

Some neoconservative theorists posit that invading Iraq will plant the seed of democracy in the Middle East. "When there is a democratic Iraq— and that is our goal— an Iraq that truly cares for the welfare of its own people, it won't only be the people of Iraq who benefit from that. It will be the whole world and very much the region," a deluded U.S. Deputy Defense Secretary Paul Wolfowitz claimed on July 17. "Turkey stands to benefit enormously when Iraq becomes a normal country."

Remember, that's what they said about Afghanistan in October. Now Osama, Mullah Omar and the Taliban are running loose in Pakistani Kashmir, radical Islamist movements are on the rise in the former Soviet republics of Central Asia, and U.S. Special Forces are personally guarding Afghan president Hamid Karzai, a despised and ridiculed American puppet whose bribed soldiers can't be trusted not to kill him, much less defend their Kabul city-state. As bad as the Taliban were, the thugs who replaced them may be even worse.

And getting rid of Saddam could lead to even-more-apocalyptic consequences.

Saddam's principal opponents are Iranian-backed Shiite groups and 20 million Sunni Kurds whose *peshmerga* fighters are struggling to create an independent Kurdish homeland comprising northern Iraq, southeastern Turkey and extreme northwestern Iran. The Shiite Supreme Council for the Islamic Revolution in Iraq (SCIRI), the Kurdistan Democratic Party (KDP) and the Patriotic Union of Kurdistan (PUK) agree that we ought to depose Saddam, but no one wants another strongman to replace him. "Our viewpoint regarding regime change is that it has to be at the hands of the Iraqi people. We will not permit there to be foreign interference, whatever its nature, in orchestrating this change," SCIRI's Mohammad al-Hariri says.

Most experts expect Iraq to disintegrate into some form of civil war after an overthrow of Saddam's oppressive Baath Party. From 1994 to 1998 the KDP and PUK fought a brutal war over control of the "no-fly zone" created by the American-led allies to protect Iraqi Kurds north of the 36th parallel. And a Turkish Kurdish group, the Kurdistan Workers' Party (PKK), has split off from Iraqi Kurds as it launches guerrilla attacks within Turkey. A post-Saddam power vacuum will encourage the Iraqi Kurds to fight for the spoils within Iraq, with the winner taking on the Shiites. Iran would likely evict its own Kurds, most of whom arrived as refugees from the Gulf War, while arming the Shiites. Just this month, 2,000 PUK troops fought pitched street battles against Islamist guerrillas of the Jund al-Islam group, leaving at least twenty dead in the northern Iraqi city of Halabja. And Turkey, which has already lost thirty thousand lives in its own Kurdish civil war, will undoubtedly suffer a renewed drive for a free and independent Kurdistan carved out of its mountainous east to join whatever Kurdish state emerges from a shattered postwar Iraq.

European and Middle Eastern, secular and Islamic, Turkey is the economically fragile strategic linchpin that holds together eastern Europe and the Balkans. If Turkey falls apart, all hell will break loose between Muslim separatists and Slavic nationalists in what's left of Yugoslavia and Albania. Gulf War 2 could ultimately lead to millions of deaths spread across three time zones.

Opinion of the United States is now at an all-time low among Muslims. One reason is our continued support of Israel's military campaign against the Palestinian Authority. Another is that we replaced what was seen as the world's purest Muslim regime, the Taliban, with with one led by an oil-company stooge. Going after Iraq will make matters worse. Why give radical anti-American Islamists even more political ammunition with which to recruit suicide bombers and attract the financial donations that fund their assaults?

The administration calls attention to Iraq's "weapons of mass destruction," but a former U.N. weapons inspector says that Iraq possesses neither nuclear nor biological devices. (Of course, no one ever calls upon the U.S. to account for *its* weapons of mass destruction. White male Protestants are presumably more trustworthy than swarthy male Sunnis.) If and when Iraq attacks its neighbors or American interests, U.S. retribution may be justified. Until then, the current combination of weekly bombing raids and devastating economic sanctions should serve as sufficient punishment for whatever it is that Saddam did to offend delicate American sensibilities.

As if it wasn't bad enough that we have no moral justification for or strategic interest in attacking Iraq, the Bushies' irresponsible war talk is sabotaging an economy already battered by accounting scandals, the dot-com hangover and fleeing foreign investment. War rhetoric and the resulting increased threat of terrorist attacks against the U.S. are driving up oil prices and making markets more volatile, says Allen Sinai, chief global economist at Decision Economics in Boston. "An invasion of Iraq raises a huge number of unanswered questions, and that kind of uncertainty is deadly for financial markets." Oil is now going for about $26 per barrel, up from $22 in January— before Bush dubbed Iraq part of an Axis of Evil. Given that Iraq produces four percent of the world's oil supply, a jump like that, at a thirty percent per annum rate, boosts gasoline, heating and transportation costs significantly, slamming the two-thirds of our economy that is dependent upon consumer spending. And the more the Bushies trash talk about the big ass-whuppin' they're going to give Saddam, the more oil prices will rise. "In the oil market, it's just starting to dawn on people that something big might be happening," says Roger Diwan, managing director of Petroleum Finance Co., a Washington consulting firm.

As we saw during World War II, defense spending can spur economic growth— but only if the war and the government spending to fight it are long and sustained. "In what is likely to be a reasonably quick and decisive operation, there isn't going to be time for a war economy to develop," asserts Anthony Cordesman, an analyst at the Center for Strategic and International Studies in Washington.

Do the Kurds deserve a homeland? Sure. Would Iraq be better off without Saddam? Probably. But if we're smart, we won't be the ones to blow over this particular house of cards. We have too much to lose and too little to gain in the mess that may eventually ensue.

Impossible Promises on Iraq

Bush administration officials have told key lawmakers not to expect a U.S. attack on Iraq before the fall elections, allowing time for Congress to debate the possibility of war. Senior administration officials gave the assurances in private conversations with senators planning a series of hearings that begin today into a possible U.S. attack on Iraq. The officials said there would be no "October surprise"—a sudden attack before the November 5 congressional elections to remove Iraqi leader Saddam Hussein.

The assurances square with Pentagon estimates that it would take until early next year to have the weapons, intelligence and forces in place to take on Iraq's 375,000-man army. One key factor: U.S. soldiers can't fight in Iraq's summer or autumn heat wearing protective gear against chemical or biological weapons attack.

—John Diamond, USA Today, July 30, 2002

OCTOBER 22, 2002—Never mind that attacking Iraq without provocation would be immoral. Forget that the Bush Administration has released no evidence that Iraqi President Saddam Hussein has "weapons of mass destruction" or that he intends to use them. Let's even ignore official Axis of Evil™ member North Korea's admission that it has developed nuclear weapons in a blatant violation of a 1994 agreement.

"The reality of the United States using force unilaterally against North Korea is extremely difficult, if not impossible," notes Daniel Pinkston, a Korea specialist at the Monterey Institute for International Studies. "[North Korea] is a little bit on the back burner." And yet Iraq is probably less of a threat than North Korea. Iraq, however, possesses an estimated 112.5 billion barrels in proven oil reserves—the world's second-largest stash. North Korea has mud. And rocks.

Guess who we're going to invade?

There's no point taking on Iraq unless we can establish a stable puppet regime in Baghdad after we win. An Iraqi civil war would cause those precious energy reserves to be split into Kurdish and non-Kurdish zones, which makes maintaining the country's territorial integrity after Saddam essential if we want to fully exploit all that oil and natural gas. Finally, a pro-American post-Saddam government won't stand a chance of garnering popular support unless the damage created by a decade of economic sanctions and the looming

"liberation" is quickly repaired.

"If the U.S. is going to take responsibility for removing the current leadership [of Iraq]," Middle East expert Phebe Marr told the Senate Foreign Relations Committee in August, "it should assume that it cannot get the results it wants on the cheap." Marr warned that there will be "retribution, score-settling and bloodletting" as a vengeful Shiite majority reacts to the end of Saddam Hussein's Sunni-dominated regime. Turkey, worried that its own suppressed Kurds might revolt in an attempt to join their Iraqi brethren, might invade. A post-Saddam power vacuum will offer a tempting opportunity for Iran to influence—i.e., arm—fellow Shiites across the border. The U.S. will have to defend Iraq's borders against both Turkey and Iran. In short, to successfully execute this war and its messy aftermath will require lots of troops, money and time.

Don't forget Afghanistan. Any planning for invading Iraq must take into account the lessons of our last—and as yet unconcluded—war in Muslim Asia.

Less than a year ago, the U.S. was promising not to abandon post-Taliban Afghanistan as it had after the 1989 Soviet withdrawal. "Chairman Karzai," Bush told the U.S.-installed Afghan president in January, "I reaffirm to you today that the United States will continue to be a friend to the Afghan people in all the challenges that lie ahead."

Months later, that pledge lies in tatters.

Far from carrying out a "Marshall Plan for Afghanistan," a crusade so loftily proposed during the heady days after the defeat of the Taliban, the U.S. has dedicated a piddling $296 million to rebuild the world's poorest, most war-torn nation. Secretary of State Colin Powell concedes that even an original cost estimate of $4.5 billion would not have been "nearly as good as it needs to be."

Karzai's Foreign Minister Abdullah Abdullah, warning that his government is on the verge of financial collapse, reports that Afghanistan requires at least $20 billion for rebuilding. As it is, Karzai hasn't even been able to pay Afghan government workers their salaries—on average a mere $20 per month. Not an inch of roadway has been paved in the whole country. The U.N. food program estimates that twenty-five percent of Afghanistan's 16 million people will suffer from starvation this winter.

Unsurprisingly, farmers are back in the heroin business. "We are growing poppies because of poverty, because the government pledged to pay us for destroying our harvests, but did not pay us anything," farmer Abdul Malik tells Reuters near the Helmandi provincial capital of Lashkargah. "We are growing it because not one school, or hospital, or road has been rehabilitated here as promised."

Only 8,000 U.S. soldiers are currently stationed in Afghanistan—less than three percent of the 300,000 the Army says that it needs to properly "Marshall Plan" the country—and most of those are traipsing through the mountains near Khost in search of al-Qaedans who fled for Pakistan in 2001. Actual "peacekeeping" is limited to Kabul; the vast majority of Afghans live under the same feudal warlords whose brutality led to the rise of the Taliban in the mid 1990s. Rape, robbery and violent clashes are routine.

We did Afghanistan on the cheap, and it shows. The place is such a mess that the main objective of the American invasion—building a trans-Afghan pipeline to carry landlocked Caspian oil and gas to the Indian Ocean—will likely never be realized.

We won the war but we lost the peace. Will we do the same thing in Iraq?

Count on it.

After Saddam, the Deluge

President Bush's case against Saddam Hussein, outlined in a tele-
vised address to the nation on Monday night, relied on a slanted
and sometimes entirely false reading of the available U.S. intelli-
gence, government officials and analysts claimed yesterday.
"Basically, cooked information is working its way into high-level
pronouncements and there's a lot of unhappiness about it in intel-
ligence, especially among analysts at the CIA," said Vincent
Cannistraro, the CIA's former head of counter-intelligence.
                    —Julian Borger, UK Guardian, October 9, 2002

NOVEMBER 5, 2002—When George W. Bush wanted the Taliban out, he issued an ulti-matum: give up Osama or face the consequences. Mullah Omar and his grim band of Islamist yahoos were fearsome literalists; in a now-forgotten last-ditch attempt to keep their jobs, they offered to turn over bin Laden. But Bush didn't really want bin Laden, of course—he just wanted the Taliban gone. Days later, bombs began raining on Afghanistan. Bushian ultimata are merely eviction notices.

A year later Saddam Hussein is sitting through the same "let's make this look good" rit-ual. Bush doesn't want arms inspectors. He wants Iraq. Nothing Saddam does or offers to do will make any difference. War was likely before Election Day, but now the Republican sweep makes it inevitable.

Bombs will fall. People will die. We Americans will mostly just care about the Americans who die—and we won't be upset about them for very long. And what happens after the last oil-well fire has been extinguished? We'll be like a dog that finally catches a passing car. What the hell does he do with it? And what will we do with the oil-rich, frac-tious, mountainous, marshy, desert country full of Sunnis, Shiites and Kurds once we final-ly oust Saddam?

The U.S. didn't put much serious advance planning into who would run post-Taliban Afghanistan (remember King Zahir Shah?). Now we're about to take over Iraq without hav-ing clue one about what kind of government to install or who will be in charge of it.

In 1998 Congress passed the Iraqi Liberation Act. Under that law the U.S. officially rec-ognizes six Iraqi groups as possible alternatives to Saddam Hussein's regime: two Kurdish militias currently running Iraq's northern "no-fly zone," the Iraqi National Accord, the Iraqi National Congress, the Teheran-based Supreme Council of the Islamic Revolution in Iraq (SCIRI) and a small Hashemite monarchist group.

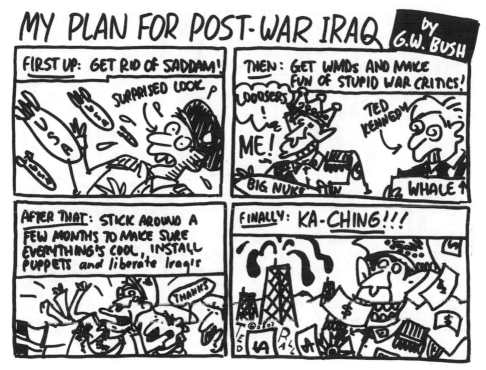

Riven by its own turf battles, the Bush Administration is unable and unwilling to declare which—if any of these outfits should rule Iraq after the coming war. On October 28, a new conservative daily newspaper, the *New York Sun,* reported that the administration was considering naming a special presidential envoy to the Iraqi opposition. But, the *Sun* wrote, "The matter has become entangled in the vicious policy struggle between the Pentagon and the Vice President's office, on the one hand, and the State Department and the CIA, on the other hand."

This is what things have come to: within the Bush Administration the State Department and CIA are the reasonable moderates. They prefer giving U.N. weapons inspectors a real chance to avoid war and deny that there's any connection between Saddam and al-Qaeda. (Al-Qaeda operatives are active in Iraq, but only in Kurdistan, where Saddam's government has no control.) They back the Shiite-aligned SCIRI and the Iraqi National Accord, which tried to depose Saddam in a 1998 coup attempt. The Defense Department and Dick Cheney, on the other hand, are the hawks. They favor a pliant umbrella organization, the Iraqi National Congress, to manage the locals while the U.S. pumps out the oil.

"Tensions are so high," reports the *Sun,* "that ground rules have been established banning representatives of the State Department from meeting with representatives of the Iraqi opposition without a representative of the Defense Department present, and, likewise, banning representatives of the Defense Department from meeting with the Iraqi opposition without a representative of the State Department present."

Even within one fiefdom, U.S. officials have a hard time keeping their story straight. "Americans agreed that the future Iraqi government should be an elected government,"

SCIRI leader Mohammed Baqir al-Hakim said on October 21. "They also agreed that a military ruler wouldn't work." SCIRI's main supporter, Secretary of State Colin Powell, however, told the Associated Press exactly the opposite: "The United States," the AP quoted Powell, "is considering a model for postwar Iraq that resembles Japan after World War II, when Japan was occupied by an American-led military government."

Lost amongst the internal squabbling is the real possibility that none of the six approved groups may prove any better than the violently autocratic Saddam Hussein. Human Rights Watch accuses both Kurdish militias of "a wide variety of human rights violations, including the arbitrary detention of suspected political opponents, torture, and extrajudicial executions," as well as ethnic cleansing. Kurdish policy towards women is indistinguishable from that of the Taliban; the Kurds take hard-line Islamism even further by endorsing the "honor killing" of women who have sex outside marriage—even if they have been raped.

The Taliban, bleeding-heart liberals by comparison, at least stoned the *rapists* to death.

All six approved groups subscribe to conservative Islam. Several endorse the same Sharia law used to justify stonings and *burqas* in Afghanistan, all would curtail the rights of Iraqi women (who, under Saddam, enjoy the most freedom of women in any Arab state) and only one can be called pro-American. Like Afghanistan's Northern Alliance, these factions will fight one another as soon as they get the chance.

"Our objective for the long term in Iraq would be to establish a broad-based representative and democratic government," said Bush foreign policy adviser and Special Envoy to Afghanistan, Zalmay Khalilzad. But most analysts believe that replacing Saddam with any, some or all of these groups will only hasten the balkanization of Iraq. That is, after all, exactly what happened after the U.S. invaded Afghanistan.

Tell us again; heck, tell us even once—why are we about to do this thing?

Droit du Seigneur:
Bush as God

American citizens working for al-Qaeda overseas can legally be targeted and killed by the CIA under President Bush's rules for the war on terrorism, U.S. officials say. The authority to kill U.S. citizens is granted under a secret finding signed by the president after the September 11 attacks that directs the CIA to covertly attack al-Qaeda anywhere in the world. The authority makes no exception for Americans, so permission to strike them is understood rather than specifically described, officials said.

These officials said the authority will be used only when other options are unavailable. Military-like strikes will take place only when law enforcement and internal security efforts by allied foreign countries fail, the officials said. Capturing and questioning al-Qaeda operatives is preferable, even more so if an operative is a U.S. citizen, the officials said, speaking on the condition of anonymity. Any decision to strike an American will be made at the highest levels, perhaps by the president.

—Associated Press, December 4, 2002

DECEMBER 10, 2002—First he appointed himself president. Now George W. Bush has declared himself God.

As Americans begin their third year of Supreme Court-ordered political occupation, Bush has just signed an impressive new executive order. You may be surprised to learn that it grants him the right to order your execution. No judge, jury or lawyer. No chance to prove your innocence. One stroke of Bush's pen, and bang—you're dead.

Not even your American citizenship, according to Bush, will save your life if and when he decides to kill you. The only reason you're reading this right now—instead of meeting the Entity Formerly Known as God—is that neither Bush nor one of his "high-level officials" has yet signed a piece of paper declaring you an "enemy combatant." Once they do the paperwork, Administration officials assert, they have the right to murder you.

Bush's secret assassination directive surfaced on December 3, when reporters asked about the November 3 Central Intelligence Agency rub-out of alleged al-Qaeda operatives riding in a car in Yemen. Langley fired a Hellfire missile from a remote-controlled

Predator drone into the vehicle, blowing up several men. The CIA later discovered that an American citizen, Kamal Derwish, had inadvertently been killed in the resulting inferno.

"No constitutional questions are raised here," asserted National Security Advisor Condoleezza Rice, stretching credulity even more than usual. Officials claim that a loophole in Bush's order authorizing the CIA to "covertly attack al-Qaeda all over the world" validates Derwish's murder. Since this sneaky directive makes exception neither for Americans nor American soil, these guys say, you and I have no more rights than the now-deceased, not-presumed-innocent Kamal Derwish.

Your life, liberty and the pursuit of happiness are now officially subject to George W. Bush's personal judgment—or whim.

The war on terrorism isn't a war, it's a cheesy public service announcement, like the "war on poverty" and the "war on drugs." Like those old un-won campaigns, it involves no declaration of war, no defined enemy, no front. And like them it will gradually fade into embarrassing irrelevance. "Can you believe it?" future citizens will marvel. "People actually took that crap seriously!" In the meantime, America's Gang of Four—Bush, Cheney, Rumsfeld and Ashcroft—have brilliantly exploited the nebulousness of nullity. Having no enemy means that *anyone* can be declared the enemy. Having no battleground means that the battleground is anywhere and everywhere. "The Bush Administration and al-Qaeda together have defined the entire world as a battlefield," writes the Associated Press' John J. Lumpkin.

While the CIA has targeted American citizens in the past, those killings were officially sanctioned only when the person in question was considered an immediate threat to American lives. Scott L. Silliman, director of the Duke University Center on Law, Ethics

and National Security, asks: "Could you put a Hellfire missile into a car in Washington, D.C. under the same theory? The answer is yes, you could."

Never mind that anyone driving on the Beltway could just as easily be pulled over by the cops. Like the medieval lords who wielded the right of life and death over their subjects, our Texan warlord now claims the *droit du seigneur* over the American people—whether he needs it or not.

Under his legalized assassination mandate, Bush could theoretically declare the 2004 Democratic nominee an "enemy combatant," Hellfire his campaign bus and coast to reelection unopposed. It would be a hell of a lot easier than preparing for debates.

Granted, it's unlikely that CIA missiles will begin raining down on Berkeley or other liberal burgs anytime soon. Murdering Muslims, even those with U.S. citizenship, is one thing; offing "ordinary" Americans is another. As has been the case with previous Bushie infringements on fundamental civil rights—electronic eavesdropping, jailing people without trial or a visit by a lawyer—most citizens believe themselves safe simply by virtue of their not being terrorists.

They may be right. They might be wrong. Whatever, it's all in the hands of the executioner-in-chief now.

Iraq: Another War, Still Zero Proof

*"We have known for many years that Saddam Hussein is seeking
and developing weapons of mass destruction."*
—Senator Ted Kennedy (D-MA), September 27, 2002

DECEMBER 24, 2002—Eleven days after September 11, 2001, Secretary of State Colin Powell promised to release proof that al-Qaeda and Osama bin Laden were guilty of planning and executing the attacks on New York and Washington. "We will put before the world, the American people, such a persuasive case that there will be no doubt when that case is presented that it is al-Qaeda, led by Osama bin Laden, who has been responsible," Powell told ABC News.

National Security Advisor Condoleeza Rice, speaking a few channels over on CNN, echoed Powell's pledge. "Clearly we do have evidence, historical and otherwise, about the relationship to the al-Qaeda network to what happened on September 11th," Rice said on September 22, 2001. "We will begin to lay out that evidence and we will do it with friends, allies and the American people and others."

Afghanistan, along with Pakistan, had hosted al-Qaeda training camps. Al-Qaeda, Bush said, had attacked us. So we bombed Afghanistan. The Bush Administration spent the next three months overseeing the dropping of explosives, killing an estimated 10,000 Taliban soldiers and at least 3,500 Afghan civilians. During the year since we installed a puppet ruler, Hamid Karzai, as interim Afghan president, at least thirty-six American soldiers have lost their lives defending Karzai's fragile regime.

So where's Rice's "evidence, historical and otherwise," confirming that al-Qaeda carried out 9/11? Where is Powell's "persuasive case"? The Bushies, as usual, are keeping mum. We, the American people, have yet to see the slightest shred of evidence tying Osama bin Laden, Mullah Omar, Michael Jackson or the Easter Bunny to the attacks.

Fifteen months and still no proof! There are only three logical explanations for Bush's failure to produce the goods:

Al-Qaeda and the Taliban had nothing to do with 9/11. Possible, but unlikely. Al Qaeda certainly had some role, though they didn't carry out the attacks themselves.

What with the war and all, the Bushies simply forgot to write up a report. Impossible. If proof existed, the Administration would have released it to make people like me shut up.

The evidence is circumstantial at best. Now we're talking. More likely than not,

American intelligence strongly suspects bin Laden et al. but can't prove his guilt beyond a reasonable doubt.

Police detectives are repeatedly frustrated by this dilemma. What do you do when you know in your gut that a suspect is guilty, but you don't have enough evidence to press charges? The answer is painfully obvious: you let the bastard walk. In a society based upon law, evidence must be sufficiently compelling in order to charge a defendant, much less convict him. To settle for less is to sacrifice the essential principle of our nation that holds that everyone—even radical Islamists—is presumed innocent.

George W. Bush, an unscrupulous man whose arrogant contempt for the law elevated him to the White House, despises basic American values. He acted as Afghanistan's judge, jury and executioner—without even possessing sufficient proof to charge bin Laden in an American court.

Now, however, Bush is paying a price for the decision not to lay his cards on the table regarding Afghanistan. While 90 percent of voters say they don't doubt that Saddam Hussein is developing weapons of mass destruction, 72 percent told a *Los Angeles Times* poll on December 15 that Bush has not yet provided enough evidence to justify starting a war against Iraq. This figure includes many Republicans who otherwise support Bush's policies.

Most Americans have a gut feeling that Iraq has WMDs. But they don't think a gut feeling is sufficient cause to go to war.

Here we go again. Does the U.S. really possess proof, as it claims, that Saddam is up to no good? Or does it merely *suspect*—in other words, have a gut feeling—that Iraqi scientists are cooking up smallpox bombs hundreds of feet beneath the desert? The

American people aren't being allowed to see the evidence excusing the bloody war about to be waged in their name. Nor are the prospective allies whose help—and young men— we are requesting. "To say that we know but we won't tell you is not very persuasive," Sergey Lavrov, the Russian Ambassador to the United Nations, said. "It's not a poker game where you call your cards and call the other's bluff."

Incredibly, Bush even resisted turning over intelligence data on Iraqi weapons to the U.N., information that might help inspectors prove Saddam was violating the 1991 cease-fire agreement. Approval ratings for an American war on Iraq are slipping. Unless he coughs up definitive proof of Iraqi wrongdoing or calls off the whole thing, this latest oil-driven military misadventure could become Bush's political Waterloo.

A Dog of a War

This article originally appeared in The Stranger

JANUARY 29, 2003—As the United States prepares to launch its second war of the new millennium, it may be useful to note that pacifism is, like anarchy and libertarianism, a meaningless and foolish ideology. A world without war would be a world without human beings; organized mass killing is an inherent reality, the ultimate fall-back position for those who can't or won't negotiate for what they want with those who have it. Peace is ideal, but will people ever give it a chance.

While war involves wholesale slaughter and pointless destruction, sometimes war can be good. More precisely, war can be justified under certain circumstances.

Self-defense, for instance. When your country is invaded, you have the right to kill the aggressor's soldiers and, if things go favorably, to destroy the territory of the attacking nation-state after you drive them back across their borders.

Another acceptable war aim is the liberation of oppressed peoples. It's immoral for the world to stand by and watch as a government, whether by action or inaction, presides over the systematic imposition of misery on its citizens. However, liberation is a tricky endeavor. Often the people the invaders want to save view them as just that—invaders bent on domination and exploitation. Example: While I consider George W. Bush to be a dangerous man who seized power extraconstitutionally, I wouldn't trust an invading army whose purported goal was to "liberate" the United States from his illegitimate rule. Because whether to retain or get rid of the Bush junta is an affair for Americans and not foreigners, I would fight to defend America's border (see self-defense, above).

Even wars of transparent aggression are sold to the public as acts of self-defense and selfless liberation. As Nazi Germany prepared to invade Czechoslovakia in 1936, Hitler claimed that ethnic Germans living in the Sudetenland were being abused by the Czech authorities. In 1939, German officials dragged political prisoners to a German-Polish frontier checkpoint, dressed them in Polish army uniforms, and shot them to death. They distributed film of the bodies as "evidence" of a Polish invasion that had to be "repelled."

War is a manifestation of that most primitive of animal instincts: greed. Someone has something—land, food, minerals, oil, a deep-water port—that someone else wants. Often the side that wants can only achieve its ends by killing the side that has.

Of all the wars we have fought, we Americans are most morally confident of our role in World War II. Three despotic empires responsible for the murder of nearly one hundred million people were overthrown, their violent ideologies were bankrupted and a billion souls

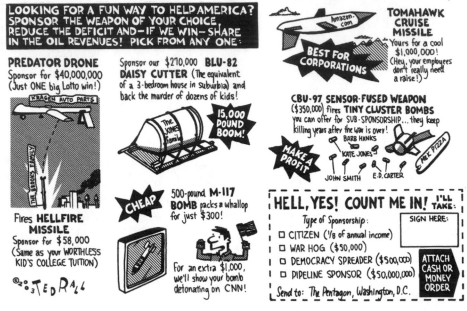

were liberated from oppression. Though the U.S. had a nebulous claim to self-defense in the Pacific—Japan had bombed Hawaii, a far-flung outpost which American Marines had themselves seized by force a half-century before—there was no imminent danger of an already overextended German empire extending its western front across the Atlantic. Furthermore, interest in ending the Holocaust or feeding starving European children did not motivate America's decision to fight. As memos and other documents authored by Franklin Roosevelt in the National Archives prove, American leaders entered the war because they sought to create a power vacuum to open European markets to American goods. Germany had something—Europe—that we wanted. Liberation, and ending genocide, were happy by-products of that effort.

Were we right to fight World War II? Maybe. Were the results, on balance, positive? Absolutely.

After a year spent floating a variety of bizarre pretexts for invading the Republic of Iraq—including Saddam Hussein's alleged role in an assassination attempt on his father—George W. Bush has settled on those time-honored classics: liberation and self-defense. In truth, Saddam has something—oil and a nice spot for U.S. military bases—that Bush wants. But that's not how he puts it.

"Should Saddam Hussein seal his fate by refusing to disarm, by ignoring the opinion of the world, you will be fighting not to conquer anybody, but to liberate people," Bush told U.S. troops earlier this year. "No matter what their oppressors may say, the people of Iraq have no love for tyranny. Like all human beings, they desire and they deserve to live in liberty and to live in dignity." After first-world nations allowed Rwanda to disintegrate into chaos and genocide, Bill Clinton used similar rhetoric to justify military action in Somalia,

Haiti and Yugoslavia.

Bush's twist on the self-defense excuse takes post-9/11 nationalist paranoia to dazzling new heights. Banking on lingering desires to prevent future September 11s no matter what, Bush asks Americans and allied leaders to subscribe to an unprecedented Bush Doctrine under which we can attack anyone, anywhere, any time we feel threatened.

"Deterrence, the promise of massive retaliation against nations, means nothing, against shadowy, terrorist networks with no nation or citizens to defend," Bush said in June. "Containment is not possible when unbalanced dictators with weapons of mass destruction can deliver those weapons on missiles or secretly provide them to terrorists' allies. We must take the battle to the enemy, disrupt his plans and confront the worst threats before they emerge. And our security will require all Americans to be forward-looking and resolute, to be ready for preemptive action when necessary to defend our liberty and to defend our lives."

Saddam Hussein may have weapons of mass destruction, Bush argues. He may be planning to use them against the U.S. or its allies. Alternatively, he may give or sell them to terrorist organizations like al-Qaeda (never mind that radical Islamist groups despise Iraq as a corrupt, liberal, secular state). Thus the only way to positively preclude that possibility—remember, it is only a possibility—is to invade Iraq, overthrow Saddam Hussein and turn the country upside down in search of those (possible) weapons so that they can (possibly) be destroyed.

Preemption is a radical departure from the history of a nation that thinks of itself as fighting only to defend itself and its closest allies. Although the U.S. technically reserved the right to launch a first nuclear strike during the Cold War, in practice both diplomats and military planners relied on a principle of Mutual Assured Destruction under which neither the U.S. nor the Soviet Union would be motivated to attack first. Lyndon Johnson's claims, later proven untrue, that North Vietnam had shelled American ships convinced Congress to support the Tonkin Gulf Resolution that began the Vietnam War in earnest. LBJ marketed Vietnam as a blend of vengeance, self-defense and ideological proxy warfare. It all boiled down to standing up for America's friends and America's way of life.

A country that declares its right to launch preemptive strikes becomes a danger to its neighbors. The current North Korean crisis began as a direct result of the Bush Doctrine. Leader Kim Jong Il is so scared that he's next on Bush's "regime change" checklist that he reactivated his country's nuke program as a bargaining chip, says Donald Gregg, a former U.S. Ambassador to South Korea and Seoul station chief for the CIA. "I think their military is frightened by us." If we have the right to take over other countries to prevent them from attacking first, it logically follows—from their point of view—that they have the same right to attack us. Our enemies fear us more, hate us more and are more likely to hit us first. Other nations acquire more weapons to defend themselves from us. Meanwhile, the allies who know us best, as we're seeing in the cases of France and Germany, begin to question our motives.

There's good reason for the international community, if there is such a thing, to distrust Bush Administration claims that its looming war with Iraq is an act of self-defense. "We know [Saddam Hussein has] got ties with al-Qaeda," Bush claimed in November. A few days later, British Foreign Secretary Jack Straw—a staunch ally—called Bush a liar. "What I'm asked is if I've seen any evidence of that. And the answer is: I haven't."

There is no link between the Iraqi government and al-Qaeda or any other Islamist

group. They're ideological, cultural and political polar opposites. Nonetheless, Bush repeated this laughable, undocumented allegation in his 2003 State of the Union address. "Imagine those nineteen hijackers with other weapons and other plans, this time armed by Saddam Hussein," Bush asked. "It would take one vial, one canister, one crate slipped into this country to bring a day of horror like none we have ever known."

"Imagine" it? Fantasy will have to do, since it won't happen.

No one seriously believes that Iraq intends to attack the United States or anyone else. Partitioned into a de facto Kurdish homeland and two unilaterally-imposed "no fly" zones, its economy wrecked by a decade of trade sanctions and its infrastructure degraded by weekly bombing sorties so routine they don't rate a mention on CNN, the Iraqi government can't afford more misadventures like its conflicts with Iran and Kuwait. Past performance may not guarantee future returns, but twelve years of Iraq offering no more resistance than halfhearted anti-aircraft fire ought to count for something.

Polls show that the public support for blasting Iraqis into smithereens shoots up from lackluster to massive—only if and when Bush can cough up proof that Hussein has nukes, bacterial nasties or poison gases and plans to use them on us. Administration heavies have implied that they have the goods on Saddam. So where is the evidence? "The burden of proof is on [Iraq], if they want to create confidence that they do not have any weapons of mass destruction left," says U.N. Weapons Inspector Hans Blix. "The burden of proof is not on us to run around in every house in Iraq to search for it." But no one, as Blix knows, can prove a negative.

Can anyone doubt that, if proof existed, it would have been released months ago? What conceivable reason could there be for withholding the "smoking gun" from a public that wants only that to support a war? There is no such evidence.

Even if Saddam Hussein had nukes, he wouldn't be able to use them—at least not against the United States. That's because Iraq doesn't possess any means of accurately delivering weapons to distant targets. Iraq's SCUD C missiles are only considered reliable to a maximum range of 300 miles; its Al Hussein rocket might make it 400 miles. The only way Hussein can nuke New York is via FedEx.

That leaves American allies, specifically Israel and Saudi Arabia, as the only possible victims of future attacks. Whether or not we have a duty to defend Israel, we have already provided it with upgraded Patriot anti-rocket missile systems, and it has already demonstrated its willingness to strike preemptively by bombing an Iraqi nuclear power plant in 1981. Given the Saudis' role in financing Islamist Wahhabism throughout the Middle East and

Central Asia, shouldn't young Americans let the Saudis die for their own corrupt monarchy?

It isn't necessary to wallow in conjecture when considering the likely outcome of a U.S. war on Iraq. Our invasion of Afghanistan provides us with a uniformly dismal record of lies, broken promises, ineptitude and ill intent that augurs poorly for the coming Iraqi incursion.

Bush's official reasons for bombing and imposing regime change on Afghanistan closely parallel those he's now using for Iraq. A dangerous man, terrorist Osama bin Laden, had to be neutralized. The regime that harbored him, the Taliban, threatened its neighbors. As a bonus, it would be replaced with a liberal Western-style democracy.

Bush promised that U.S. forces would stay in Afghanistan as long as it took and spend as much money as necessary to rebuild the country and establish law and order under a strong central government.

Like LBJ's phony Tonkin Gulf incident, however, Bush's excuses for going after the Taliban turned out to be untrue. Weeks after the world's richest country began bombing the poorest on October 6, 2001, the Bushies were retroactively justifying a strategy (bombing rather than invading over land) that ensured bin Laden's escape to Pakistani Kashmir—*We're coming! Next week! Next month!*—by claiming that capturing the head of al-Qaeda "dead or alive" hadn't really been a main objective after all. "I just don't know whether we'll be successful [in capturing bin Laden]," said Donald Rumsfeld on October 25.

Though the Taliban hosted al-Qaeda training camps, Pakistan—an American ally— had many more. September 11 had been carried out by Saudis and Egyptians, some of whom happened to have trained in Afghanistan; attacking the Taliban to get even with or neutralize anti-American Islamists was like bombing Yale to get at Bush. It was a distraction, a sideshow. It was bullshit.

What America did with its first Bush-era colony should give pause to those inclined to believe its promises to do well by a post-Saddam Iraq. Experts estimated that a true Marshall Plan for Afghanistan—occupation forces to enforce law and order, creating a real government, construction of basic infrastructure—would have required at least 250,000 permanently stationed American troops and $25 billion spent over five years. Afghan President (more accurately, Mayor of Kabul) Hamid Karzai puts the cost at $45 billion over 10 years.

Instead of a U.S.-led attempt to rebuild, Afghanistan got five percent of a Marshall Plan and a country allowed to disintegrate into the 1995-style warlordism that spurred Afghans to turn to the Taliban in the first place. "The U.S. is still giving Afghanistan roughly $300 million per year," says a disappointed former National Security Council member Robert Orr.

"That is nothing close to what the U.S. did for Europe during the Marshall Plan." No roads have been paved, no wells have been dug, no electricity has been rigged. The total U.S. force in Afghanistan is 8,000, all stationed in Karzai's Kabul city-state. Even in Kabul, the *New York Times* reports, the U.S. hasn't built a single house. Karzai can't pay his own staff.

For progressive proponents of the White House's wars on Afghanistan and Iraq, cynical economic motives for war are a minor issue. Getting rid of oppressive regimes is, by itself, a positive step; whatever comes next, they assume, is bound to be an improvement.

Indeed, the Taliban may have been the world's worst government. Their treatment of women and ethnic minorities, especially Hazarans, was genocidal. Their contempt for art and culture led them to systematically destroy their war-torn nation's cultural heritage, culminating with the dynamiting of the two giant Buddhas at Bamiyan in early 2001. Their medieval, extrajudicial system of Sharia Islamic law made public stonings and amputations the nation's only must-see entertainment.

The United States has pulled off a triumph of entropy in Afghanistan. Incredibly, we have replaced the world's worst regime with one that, from the standpoint of Afghan citizens, is even worse.

The Taliban, who came to power as anti-rapist vigilantes, did provide one major boon to Afghanistan: they restored law and order to the ninety-five percent of the country under their control. It became possible to travel the nation's roads unmolested by checkpoints manned by violent armed thugs. People went out after dark. Rapists, robbers and murderers were brutally punished.

As I witnessed in the Takhar and Kunduz provinces in November and December of 2001, the collapse of the Taliban created a power vacuum that was immediately, and remains to this day, filled by the same regional warlord-financed militias that terrorized Afghans before 1996. Around Mazar-e-Sharif, for example, the Uzbek warlord Abdul Rashid Rostum's forces have set up roadblocks where anyone who passes is robbed, raped or killed at the whim of AK-47-toting teenagers. Individual "commanders" have further subdivided the area into minute districts so that it's impossible to get around without paying them off.

There are no cops. Men walk up to each other in the streets, shoot to kill and walk away. Nothing happens. The streets empty after 5 p.m.; gunshots and the screams of victims fill the nights. Post-Taliban Afghanistan is "Mad Max" come to life.

A few girls attend newly opened schools. Music is sold in bazaars. But what good does it do to teach a woman how to read if she can be violated or murdered with impunity? Who cares about music when you risk your life by going outdoors? Law and order is the basis of civilization; without it little else matters. Under the Northern Alliance, Sharia law lives on— the "new" Afghan judiciary retains all of the mullahs who spent the Taliban period chopping off arms and stoning adulterers. Women still wear the *burqa*, not because it's the law but because they're terrified.

The Northern Alliance is the Taliban minus security.

From the U.S. perspective, Afghanistan remains as much of a threat as before. *Newsweek* reports that al-Qaeda's old training camps are back in operation. After a successful Taliban campaign to wipe out the heroin trade, Afghanistan is once again the world's leading cultivator of opium poppies used by European junkies.

Invading a sovereign state to impose "regime change" is a bad idea. If people don't like their government, whether or not to launch a revolution should be their decision. But given that you are going in, the least you can do is to do the job right.

Ultimately, the U.S. doesn't possess the political culture or national demeanor of great empire builders like the British. Rather than install military and civilian governors to manage our newly-conquered lands, we hire tin-pot puppet dictators. Rather than dispatch colonists to spread American civilization to the unwashed hordes, we stick a few thousand troops in a walled cantonment near the capital. We don't pave roads, build houses, feed people, or create jobs. We don't buy good will.

We do vaccinate children. Then they go outside, where they step on Soviet mines or pick up brightly colored canisters from American cluster bombs. At least their minced flesh is disease-free.

Like all half-assed endeavors, occupation on the cheap is the worst possible strategy. You piss off the locals without disarming them. You radicalize moderates. You get blamed for everything that goes wrong, without having enough of a budget to make anything better. That's exactly what happened in Afghanistan. Most people are hungrier, and angrier, than before. They know that, rather than bring democracy to Afghanistan, we imposed an impotent puppet government. Their rage—the rage of a fearsome people whose national pastime is the blood feud—is focused on us. Memo to future invaders: Go in, and stay in, with overwhelming force for the foreseeable future, or don't go in at all.

Needless to say—but for those of us who oppose this war, it is oddly necessary to say—Saddam Hussein is a brutal dictator. He suppresses Iraq's Shiite majority, lines the pockets of his cronies with stolen oil revenues and fills his jails with Kurds and other political opponents. Iraqis should get rid of him.

Yet the world is full of horrible despots, and Bush doesn't talk about changing *their* regimes. Pakistan's Musharraf tortured the democratically elected president he deposed in a coup d'état. Turkmenistan's Niyazov, a megalomaniacal tyrant who built a gilt 120-feet-high statue of himself in central Ashkhabat as his citizens struggle to make ends meet on an average salary of $20 a month, likes to "disappear" people he finds disagreeable. Both men are Bush's dear allies in America's "war on terror."

This isn't a war; it's a labor-management dispute. Saddam Hussein, himself a close ally of the first President Bush, gassed countless Kurds without any objection from the State Department—until he invaded Kuwait without asking permission. Just as George W. Bush never mentioned the plight of Afghan women before September 2001, he never gave a damn about oppressed Iraqis until their torment became a convenient talking point for war. The bottom line is that Saddam has something Bush wants—Iraq—and Bush is willing to kill him to get it.

We should be careful, though. Blowing up Saddam or putting him out to pasture on the French Riviera will likely replace Iraq's execrable Baath Party with something even worse.

Saddam Hussein's Iraq is, from the standpoint of women's rights, one of the most liberal Arab states in the Middle East. They hold high-ranking jobs in government and private industry and dress like Westerners. Profoundly tied into Iraq's sense of national identity is the idea, supported by socialist wealth-distribution programs and massive subsidies, that the nation's oil wealth must be enjoyed by ordinary people rather than exploited for the sole benefit of foreign corporations. These are good things. Would a Bush-backed Shiite-Kurdish puppet coalition apply similar policies? Women living in Kurdish-ruled Iraq—where, incidentally, remnants of al-Qaeda do operate—exist in a world closer to Kabul than Baghdad. And most of U.S.-backed Iraqi opposition espouse right-wing views on religion and social mores.

The 2001 U.S. invasion reduced Afghanistan to anarchic civil war. Iraq is even more fragile. Kurds will demand an independent state. Iran already funds its fellow Shiites within Iraq. Instability will spread to neighboring countries whose governments are doing their best to create fairer societies. Turkey's restless Kurdish minority will undoubtedly agitate to join their brothers across the border in Iraq. Radical Islamist groups operating within Kurdistan would try to seize power there. A Turkish civil war would send shock waves through the Balkans, Israel and Palestine. Given this scenario, American military governors would likely turn to another Iraqi strongman, a grim copy of Saddam Hussein, to hold the country together. Democracy? Not bloody likely.

War can be good, but there's no good reason to go to war in Iraq. The reasons we're being given are false, the real reasons are stupid and there's no chance we Americans will spend the time and money to repair everything we've broken after we're all done. How ironic: thousands killed, billions spent, and we'll probably never see a drop of all that oil.

The Case For the French

Want french fries on Capitol Hill? Better change that order to "freedom fries." On Tuesday, Ohio Republican Robert Ney unilaterally ordered the word "French" removed from congressional cafeteria menus to protest France's refusal to back the United States in the war against Iraq. The directive from Ney, House Administration Committee chairman, affects three Capitol Hill cafeterias that sell french fries and five that offer french toast, which now will be dubbed "freedom toast."
       —Greg Wright, Gannett News Service, March 12, 2003

MARCH 12, 2003—Who are we to be bashing the French?

The trouble began when President Jacques Chirac openly expressed the private beliefs of virtually every other world leader—that George W. Bush's desire to start an unprovoked war with Iraq is both crazy and immoral. It has quickly disintegrated into a ferocious display of American nativism that would be hilarious if its gleeful idiocy wasn't so frightening.

"Axis of Weasel," howls the *New York Post* in reaction to France and Germany's U.N. stance. A North Carolina restaurateur replaces French fries with "freedom fries." In West Palm Beach, a bar owner dumps his stock of French wine in the street, vowing to replace it with vintages from nations that support a U.S. invasion of Iraq. (Well, there's always Bulgaria.) Also in Palm Beach, a county official is working to boycott French businesses from government contracts: "France's attitude toward the United States is deplorable," says Commissioner Burt Aaronson. "It's quite possible that if we didn't send our troops there, the French people would all be speaking German."

Allied troops liberated the French in 1944. The least France could do, the French bashers argue, is show a little gratitude. They think that France should stand by—or better yet help out—when U.S. troops go to invade/liberate/whatever *other* countries. Sovereignty and self-determination are fine as mere words. But it just ain't right for a country we rescued from Nazi occupation to disagree with our policy fifty years after the fact and threaten us with a U.N. veto.

To be sure, France owed America a nice thank-you card for D-Day. But we owe them a little more. Without France, the United States wouldn't even *exist*—we would still be a British colony.

Every American schoolchild learns that a French naval blockade trapped Cornwallis' forces at Yorktown, bringing the American revolution to its victorious conclusion. But fewer

people are aware that King Louis XVI spent so much money on arms shipments to American rebels that he bankrupted the royal treasury, plunged his nation into depression and unleashed a political upheaval that ultimately resulted in the end of the monarchy. Franklin Roosevelt wrote some fat checks to save France; Louis gave up his and his wife's heads.

No two countries were closer during the 19th century. Americans named streets after the Marquis de la Fayette, Louis' liaison with our founding fathers. During the Civil War, France bankrolled the Union to neutralize British financing for the Confederacy. How many Americans remember that the Statue of Liberty was a gift from French schoolchildren?

Despite that long friendship, the French—along with Asians and overweight folks—remain one of the few groups Americans still feel free to openly insult. A recent Gallup poll shows that 20 percent fewer Americans view France favorably because of its unwillingness to go along with Bush's war on Iraq. Support for Germany, perpetrators of Nazism and the Holocaust (and which also opposes war against Iraq), holds steady at 71 percent.

Some of the contempt dates to France's quick defeat in the *blitzkrieg* of May-June 1940. "Do you know how many Frenchmen it takes to defend Paris?" joked Roy Blunt, a Republican who evidently represents the unfortunate voters of Missouri. "It's not known; it's never been tried."

Perhaps Congressman Blunt should visit the graves of the Frenchmen who lost their lives for their country during World War I (the first two-thirds of which, by the way, the U.S. sat out). One of them, my great-grandfather Jean-Marie Le Corre, died in the muddy trenches of eastern France in 1915. His death plunged my family, never comfortable to begin with, into abject poverty. His name is engraved on a memorial near a small church in Brittany. They say that he was a handsome guy, popular with the ladies and always good for

a joke. Because of him and 1.4 million other young men who sacrificed their lives for their country, Paris didn't fall.

France lost a staggering four percent of its population during the Great War. (Imagine a war that killed 11 million Americans today.) Twenty years later, in 1939, the French army still suffered from a massive manpower shortage. Demographics, lousy planning and equipment shortages—the Great Depression had also hit France—cost 100,000 French soldiers their lives during six awful weeks in 1940.

They failed to save Paris, but they died defending it.

The Bush Doctrine advocates invading weak states, imposing "regime change" and building an American empire composed of colonies whose dark-skinned races can be exploited for cheap labor. Napoleon Bonaparte, who terrorized Europe, had similar ideas. He easily outclasses our AWOL-from-the-Texas-Air-National-Guard Resident in the pure bellicosity department, but would we really choose Bonaparte over Chirac?

French-bashing is a nasty symptom of an underlying American predilection for anti-intellectualism: a society whose most popular TV show features smoky chatter between poets and novelists naturally threatens the land of football and Coors Light.

The fact is, France is a good friend and ally trying to make us see reason, and it doesn't deserve to be treated this shabbily. The United States, as led by Bush and his goons, is like a belligerent, out-of-control drunk trying to pick a fight and demanding the car keys at the same time. The French want to drive us home before we cause any more trouble, so we lash out at them, calling them rude names and impugning their loyalty. Sure, we'll be ashamed of our behavior in the morning, after the madness wears off. But will we have any friends left?

Home Invasion

Senior American and British military commanders were last night accepting the unwelcome reality that the strategy of a quick war leading to an early collapse of Saddam Hussein's regime has failed. As the U.S. nearly doubled the strength of its force by flying in a further 120,000 troops—not expected to be deployed in Iraq until the end of April—and subjecting Baghdad to the heaviest bombing for several days, British commanders admitted that their troops were nowhere near to controlling Basra, the second largest city.

General William Wallace, the U.S. army's senior commander in Iraq, said that the unexpected tactics of Iraqi fighters, and the U.S. army's stretched supply lines, were slowing down the campaign. "The enemy we're fighting is different from the one we'd war-gamed against," he told the Washington Post and New York Times.

General Sir Mike Jackson, head of Britain's army, declined to predict how long the war would last. He said that media references to coalition troops being "bogged down" were "tendentious." Iraqi forces in southern Iraq were "pinned down," he insisted. But he too acknowledged that the invading troops had not seen "displays of a welcoming population."

—Richard Norton-Taylor, UK Guardian, March 29, 2003

APRIL 1, 2003—Of course they're fighting back. This comes as no surprise to anyone who knows a little history. The question is, why did anyone expect anything else?

"The first war plan has failed," veteran war correspondent Peter Arnett told Iraqi television. NBC fired Arnett shortly thereafter, calling his statement "inappropriate and arguably unpatriotic." Of course, Arnett lost his job for speaking the obvious truth—but such is life covering, the emperor's new war.

An invasion of Iraq might not make us any friends overseas but, the Administration assured us as it dragged the country into its second of four preplanned wars, it sure as heck would be easy. No Iraqi would be willing to die for Saddam Hussein, they predicted, with the exception of a few diehard Republican Guard fanatics. Reluctant Iraqi conscripts would surrender in vast hordes, they swore; the biggest challenge our soldiers would face would be processing and housing the flood of eager white-flag wavers. Grateful women would chuck their *abayahs* into the drifting sands and sacrifice their virtue to magnificently chisel-chinned

GIs. Or at least offer them boutonnieres.

"We deluded ourselves into thinking that we would walk into Basra and they would throw flowers at us, that the Shiias would welcome us with open arms," a retired Army intelligence officer told *Newsday*. "That hasn't happened."

Though Operation Iraqi Freedom has been underway for only two weeks, Rumsfeld's "shock and awe" strategy was a flop. Pentagon strategists expected to have taken Baghdad by March 27. Best-laid plans and all that: U.S. generals, worried that they don't have enough men on the front lines, are considering whether to lay siege to Baghdad, bomb it to ruins or take it one block at a time. Basra hasn't fallen. Suicide bombers are on the loose, we're offing civilians and the Iraqi army has gone guerrilla. And we hold a mere four thousand Iraqi POWs. Only 45 Americans and Britons have died so far—compared to 112 total combat deaths in 1991—but allied casualties will soar if and when ground troops are ordered to take Baghdad.

To be sure, there have been more screw-ups this time around: crashing helicopters, a Patriot missile strike on a British fighter jet, cruise missiles that can't even hit the right *country* (Iran took two hits, Kuwait one). But there's another big difference between this invasion and 1991, when Iraq was trying to hold on to Kuwait:

This time it's personal. Iraqis are defending their homes, not newly captured territory. "We do not all love Saddam, but we do not love the United States either," an angry Iraqi man queuing up for relief packages spat at a ABC News mouthpiece. Narrow-minded ideologues like Bush and Rumsfeld can't process these two coexisting notions, seemingly contradictory, neither of which fits easily on a bumper sticker.

There are no Gallup polls in Iraq—you can't gauge popular opinion in a dictatorship.

Bush's assumption that Iraqis wanted Saddam deposed allowed him to underestimate their fighting spirit. Imagine the man's embarrassment! We'll either liberate the damned ingrates or kill them trying.

Certainly, there are Iraqis—we don't know how many—who oppose Saddam. But history is clear on this point: even Iraqis who want "regime change" don't want it imposed by an invading army, much less one from a nation whose devastating sanctions have killed hundreds of thousands over the last twelve years. The Iraqis know that we don't belong there, that we're there to steal their oil, that we can't be trusted. Like it or not, these are the reasons they're fighting for the Baath Party.

Invading armies are only greeted as liberators under one circumstance: when they're kicking out another, worse invader. History is clear on this. At the conclusion of World War II, cheering throngs greeted Allied tanks in France, Belgium and Holland. There were no such scenes in Germany or Japan. True, these original Axis of Evil nations ultimately went democratic (even if Japan became a stagnant, one-party nation), but not until after they'd been pounded into submission.

"Freedom"? Operation Iraqi Decimation is more like it.

As much as they may loathe Saddam, Iraqis are proud of their country, culture and rich history. In this respect, they are no different than we are. Millions of Americans consider Bush to be a hateful, extremist dimwit who seized power twice, once in an unconstitutional judicial coup d'état and again by using the 9/11 attacks as a pretext to expand his personal power. They call him names, like the Resident and Commander-in-Thief. But even the most passionately anti-Bush Americans would eagerly join their W-loving compatriots to fight any army that invaded the United States in the name of some theoretical "liberation."

I know I would.

How We Lost Iraq

Iraqis danced and waved the country's pre-1991 flag in central Baghdad's Firdos Square after a U.S. Marine armored recovery vehicle helped topple the square's huge statue of Iraqi President Saddam Hussein. Iraqis had begun tearing down portraits of Saddam and throwing shoes—a grave insult in the Arab world— and chipping away at the base of the statue with sledgehammers after a column of Marines advanced into the square Wednesday.
                                                   —CNN, April 9, 2003

APRIL 9, 2003—We wanted it to be true. It wasn't.

The stirring image of Saddam's statue being toppled on April 9 turns out to be fake, the product of a cheesy media op staged by the U.S. military for the benefit of cameramen staying across the street at Baghdad's Palestine Hotel. This shouldn't come as a surprise. Two of the most stirring photographs of World War II—the flag-raising at Iwo Jima and General MacArthur's stroll through the Filipino surf—were just as staged.

Anyone who has seen a TV taping knows that tight camera angles exaggerate crowd sizes, but even a cursory examination of last week's statue-toppling propaganda tape reveals that no more than 150 Iraqis gathered in Farbus Square to watch *American Marines*—not Iraqis—pull down the dictator's statue. Hailing "all the demonstrations in the streets," Defense Secretary Rumsfeld waxed rhapsodic: "Watching them," he told reporters, "one cannot help but think of the fall of the Berlin Wall and the collapse of the Iron Curtain."

Hundreds of thousands of cheering Berliners filled the streets when their divided city was reunited in 1989. Close to a million Yugoslavs crowded Belgrade at the end of Slobodan Milosevic's rule in 2000. While some individual Iraqis have welcomed U.S. troops, there haven't been similar outpourings of approval for our "liberation." Most of the crowds are too busy carrying off Uday's sofas to say thanks, and law-abiding citizens are at home putting out fires or fending off their rapacious neighbors with AK-47s. Yet Americans wanted to see their troops greeted as liberators, so that's what they saw on TV.

As it turns out, they were actually 150 *imported* art critics. The statue bashers were militiamen of the Iraqi National Congress, an anti-Saddam outfit led by one Ahmed Chalabi. The INC was flown into Iraq by the Pentagon over CIA and State Department protests. Chalabi is Rumsfeld's choice to become Iraq's next puppet president. Photos at the indispensable Information Clearing House web site (www.informationclearinghouse.info/arti-

cle2842.htm) place one of Chalabi's aides at the supposedly spontaneous outpouring of pro-American Saddam bashing at Fardus Square.

"When you are moving through this country there is [sic] not a lot of people out there and you are not sure they want us here," Sergeant Lee Buttrill gushed to ABC News. "You finally get here and see people in the street feeling so excited, feeling so happy, tearing down the statue of Saddam. It feels really good." That rah-rah BS is what Americans will remember about the fall of Baghdad—not the probability that Buttrill, part of the armed force that cordoned off the square to protect the Iraqi National Congress' actors, was merely telling war correspondents what they wanted to hear. In his critically acclaimed book *Jarhead*, Gulf War vet Anthony Swofford writes that Marines routinely lie-under orders-to gullible reporters.

ABC further reported: "A Marine at first draped an American flag over the statue's face, despite military orders to avoid symbols that would portray the United States as an occupying—instead of a liberating—force." Yet another lie. As anyone with eyes could plainly see, American tanks are festooned with more red, white and blue than a Fourth of July parade. And that particular flag was special—it was flying over the Pentagon at the time of the 9/11 attacks. The Defense Department gave it to the Marines in order to perpetuate Bush's lie that Iraq was involved in the 9/11 attacks.

Patriotic iconography is a funny thing. I've known that the Iwo Jima photo was staged for years, but it nonetheless stirs me every time I see it. Fardus Square's footage will retain its power long after the last American learns the truth.

It was a fitting end for a war waged under false pretexts by a fictional coalition led by an ersatz president. Bush never spent much time thinking about liberation, and even his exploitation is being done with as little concern as possible for the dignity of our new colo-

nial subjects.

What a difference a half-century makes! American leaders devoted massive manpower and money to plan for the occupation of the countries they invaded during World War II. What good would it do, they asked, to liberate Europe if criminals and tyrants filled the power vacuum created by the fleeing Nazis? Thousands of officers from a newly established Civil Affairs division of the U.S. Army were parachuted into France on the day after D-Day, while bullets were still flying, with orders to stop looting, establish law and order and restore essential services.

GWB is no FDR. Three weeks after the U.S. invaded Iraq, Civil Affairs was still stuck in Kuwait. Rumsfeld's war plan didn't allow for protecting museums and public buildings from looters. As priceless ancient Sumerian jewelry and Assyrian sculptures were being carried away on donkeys and carts, archeologist Raid Abdul Ridhar Muhammad tried to convince Marines manning a nearby Abrams tank to stop the looters. "I asked them to bring their tank inside the museum grounds," he told the *New York Times*. "But they refused and left."

"Stuff happens," Rummy said. "Freedom's untidy." Apparently our Defense Minister has the same taste in art as the recently desposed Taliban.

This Administration's policy of perpetual war has become a case study in entropy, the distinctly pessimistic notion that no matter how bad things get, we can figure out a way to make them worse. Entropy triumphed in Afghanistan, as the world's worst regime was replaced by dozens of thuggish warlords. The end of Saddam Hussein comes as welcome news, even if it's merely the accidental by-product of a barely disguised oil grab. But as Iraq's cities burn and its patrimony is hustled off into the black market and its women wail and the rape gangs rule the night, it's hard to escape the conclusion that we've lost this war as well.

The Moron Majority

53 percent of Americans now believe Saddam Hussein was personally involved in the September 11th terrorist attacks in the U.S., unchanged from the beginning of this month. This is somewhat higher, however, than before the start of the war in Iraq, when 45 percent thought Saddam Hussein had personal involvement in September 11th.

—CBS News, April 15, 2003

APRIL 15, 2003—Now it's official: most Americans are idiots.

Decades of budget cuts in education are finally yielding results, a fact confirmed by CNN's poll of March 16 which showed that an astonishing 51 percent of the public believe that Iraqi President Saddam Hussein was responsible for the September 11, 2001 terrorist attacks.

There is no reason to think that. None. True, George W. Bush has asserted the existence of *indirect links* between low-level al-Qaeda operatives and Iraqi intelligence officials—a lame lie repeatedly denied by the CIA—but even our professional prevaricator hasn't gone so far as to accuse Saddam of direct involvement in 9/11. Despite their increasingly tenuous grasp on reality, not even the Bush Administration's most fervent hawks deny that the secular dictator of Iraq is a mortal enemy of the Islamist extremists of al-Qaeda. No mainstream media outlet has ever reported otherwise.

So why do these pinheads think such a thing?

Simple: the official Bushie pretexts given for launching a unilateral invasion of Iraq don't stick. If Saddam was going to launch nukes or anthrax missiles in our direction, he would have done so during the last dozen years, while American warplanes were pulverizing his military installations with weekly bombing raids. He'd certainly let us have it this week, now that Bush is revving up the war he wanted all along—but he won't, because he can't.

Furthermore, no one really believes that the GOP is interested in liberating the oppressed people of Iraq. America's role in the world, after all, typically involves funding dictators—as Bush is currently doing in Saudi Arabia, Pakistan, Turkmenistan, Uzbekistan, Kazakhstan and Tajikistan—not democrats.

Like a befuddled chemistry lab student who works backwards from the answer in order to ensure the correct results, the Moron Majority have talked themselves into an excuse they can live with for a war they can't otherwise morally justify. Denial, after all, isn't just a river in Egypt.

SADDAM HUSSEIN HAS WEAPONS OF MASS DESTRUCTION THIS IS NOT ABOUT OIL OSAMA DEAD OR ALIVE TO HELL WITH THE GENEVA CONVENTIONS THIS IS A JOBLESS RECOVERY THE TAX CUT WILL BENEFIT EVERYONE WE WILL BE GREETED AS LIBERATORS

By a two-to-one margin, Americans think that their country should adhere to its tradition of attacking other countries in self-defense only, never preemptively. Thirty-seven percent say that they support an invasion of Iraq only with U.N. approval. This war against Iraq fulfills neither of these conditions, so Americans have managed to morph Bush's insinuations about a Saddam-al-Qaeda link into full-on blame.

Sure, we're killing innocent men, women and children over in Iraq. It's not self-defense, so let's just call it "vengeance for 9/11." Does that work for you? Great. Osama's gotta be laughing like a hyena now that the heat's off.

There is some good news in all this. I know, "good" is a relative term if you're reading this in a bomb shelter under Baghdad or trapped at your work station under the rubble of an office building some Islamist wired and brought down on your head. But the war on Iraq is likely to lead to the political demise of the man whose evil and illegitimate rule currently represents the greatest threat to stability and peace in the world: George W. Bush.

Win or lose, Iraq will probably be Bush's Waterloo. Victory over Saddam's armed forces is a given; just as a company's announcement of previously anticipated profits fails to deliver an uptick in stock price, military success is already assumed by the market of public opinion. That's why, even after it became evident that he'd be fighting this war alone (plus Tony Blair, minus the British public), Bush had to go ahead. His right-wing base, the part of the electorate that craves a belligerent president to protect it from future 9/11s, would have otherwise deserted him.

Even if Bush delivers a best-case scenario—quick defeat, minimal U.S. military and Iraqi civilian casualties—it won't do him any good. His supporters already expect that.

Things are most likely to go wrong when Bush can least afford it, during next year's campaign. Don't believe Kurdish promises to rejoin a federalized Iraq—they've had de facto independence for more than a decade and they're never coming back. Turkey has threatened to invade Iraqi Kurdistan, and they're leaning on their own Kurds. Hoping to neutralize its unruly neighbor, Iran is arming the Shiite majority. Civil war is more than likely.

It's impossible to predict the effects of prolonged American occupation of an Arab country; increased terrorism, regional instability and even greater Muslim hostility to the U.S. and its allies seem likely. But a failure to establish a long-term U.S. military presence throughout the country could prove even more damaging than a quick pullout. If Iraq follows Afghanistan into neglect, political disintegration and anarchy, we'll be able to count our resentful new enemies by the tens of millions.

American alliances and relations with the U.N. and NATO have been stretched to the breaking point. By launching an illegal, unsanctioned invasion of a sovereign nation, the U.S. has abandoned its moral standing. We are, by definition, a rogue state. More frightening than that, foreign leaders from Paris to Berlin to Beijing to Moscow are starting to count more on one another than on us. This means trouble for us, sure, but also for Bush as we notice our nation's loss of prestige.

As always, however, the fools will save us from themselves. The 51 percent who currently believe what is patently false will ultimately conclude that they were duped by Bush (though it's not really true). Like stupid Americans before them (those who bought into the Domino Theory, Joe McCarthy and the necessity of interning Japanese-Americans in concentration camps), they'll wonder what the hell they were thinking. And they'll have lots of time to think about it, what with not having a job and all.

Then they'll vote for an Unnamed Democrat, currently leading Bush 48 to 44 percent in the Quinnipiac poll released March 6.

Corporate Vultures Swoop Into the Killing Fields

Thousands of valuable historical items from Baghdad's main museum have been taken or destroyed by looters. Nabhal Amin, deputy director at the Iraqi National Museum, blamed the destruction on the United States for not taking control of the situation on the streets. On Saturday, Unesco—the UN's cultural agency—has urged the U.S. and Britain to deploy troops at Iraq's key archaeological sites and museums to stop widespread looting and destruction. Armed men have been roaming the streets of Baghdad since the city was taken by U.S. troops on Wednesday. Shops, government offices, presidential palaces and even hospitals have all been looted.

—BBC, April 12, 2003

APRIL 22, 2003—Iraq is going to hell. Shiites are killing Sunnis, Kurds are killing Arabs and Islamists are killing secular Baathists. Baghdad, the cradle of Western civilization, has been left to looters and rapists. As in Beirut during the 1970s, neighborhood zones are separated by checkpoints manned by armed tribesmen. The war has, however, managed to unite Iraqis in one respect: everyone loathes the United States.

Some Iraqis hate us for deposing Saddam Hussein. No dictator remains in power without the tacit support of at least some of his subjects. Now that we've committed the cardinal sin of conquest—getting rid of the old system without thinking up a new one—even those who chafed under Saddam blame us for their present misery. Others resent our Pentagon-appointed pretender, 58-year-old banker/embezzler Ahmed Chalabi. The State Department points out that Iraq's new puppet autocrat has zero support among Iraqis, having lived abroad since 1958. But who knows? Maybe he was a *really* popular kid.

Thousands of Iraqis have been reduced to poverty, raped and murdered by rampaging goons as U.S. Marines stood around and watched. Wanna guess how long it will take them to "get over it"? We watched the plunder of museums in Mosul and Baghdad safe at home with our tut-tut dismay, but Iraqis will remain outraged by the wanton devastation we wrought through war, permitted through negligence and shrugged off through arrogance. ("We didn't allow it," Rumsfeld shrugged. "It happened.") Imagine foreign troops sitting idly, laughing as hooligans trashed the Smithsonian, stole the gold from Fort Knox and burned down the Department of the Interior.

That was us in Iraq.

But let's forget this penny-ante stuff. Let the real looting begin! George W. Bush's bestest buddies, corporate executives at companies which donate money in exchange for a few rounds of golf and a few million-dollar favors, are being handed the keys to Iraq's oil fields.

Bush's brazen Genghis Khan act seems carefully calculated to confirm our worst suspicions. First he appoints retired general Jay Garner, president of a GOP-connected defense contractor, SYColeman Corp., as viceroy of occupied Iraq. "The idea is we are in Iraq not as occupiers but as liberators, and here comes a guy who has attachments to companies that provided the wherewithal for the military assault on that country," marvels David Armstrong, defense analyst at the National Security News Service.

Then Bush slips a $680 million contract to the Bechtel Group, whose Republican-oriented board has included such Reagan-era GOP luminaries as CIA director William Casey, Secretary of State George Shultz and Defense Secretary Caspar Weinberger. The deal puts the company in position to receive a big part of the *$100 billion* estimated total cost of Iraqi reconstruction. According to the Center for Responsive Politics, Bechtel gave Republican candidates, including Bush, about $765,000 in PAC, soft money and individual campaign contributions between 1999 and 2002.

Finally, refusing to accept bids from potential competitors, Bush grants a two-year, $490 million contract for Iraqi oil field repairs to Halliburton Co., the Houston-based company where Dick Cheney worked as CEO from 1995 to 2000. "It will look a lot worse if Halliburton gets the USAID [Agency for International Development] contract, too," Bathsheba Crocker, an Iraq specialist for the Center for Strategic and International Studies, warned in March. "Then it really starts looking bad." Guess what! Halliburton has since scored a piece of that $600 million USAID contract.

HEY FOREIGNERS! DON'T GET CUT OUT OF OUR NEXT POSTWAR BUSINESS GOLD RUSH— SIGN UP IN ADVANCE!

BANNED FROM BIDDING ON CONTRACTS IN IRAQ BECAUSE YOUR NATION REFUSED TO SUPPORT THE WAR? DON'T MAKE THAT MISTAKE AGAIN: MAKE YOUR RESERVATION NOW FOR *OUR NEXT WAR!*

TEHRAN SEOUL PYONGYANG

Teheran

©2003 TED RALL

SELECT THE OPTION THAT BEST FITS YOUR BUDGET:

☐ **TIMID OPPORTUNIST**   What You'll Get:

WE CAN'T SEND ANY TROOPS TO IRAN, BUT WE'LL VOTE FOR ANY U.N. RESOLUTION YOU NEED.

· NO HUMAN RIGHTS COMPLAINTS FOR 4 YEARS
· BIDDING RIGHTS ON SMALL BUSINESS DEALS
· VISIT FROM SECRETARY OF STATE OR DEFENSE

☐ **FEARFUL SUCK-UP**   What You'll Get:

ALL WE CAN SPARE YOU GUYS IS A TOKEN FORCE OF SOLDIERS WE WON'T MISS MUCH.

· BIDDING PRIORITY ON POSTWAR RECONSTRUCTION
· U.S. SCHOOLS WILL TEACH ONE CHAPTER ABOUT YOUR COUNTRY
· FREQUENT FLYER MILES (DELTA)

☐ **COALITION PARTNER**   What You'll Get:

TAKE MY ARMY! TRASH MY ECONOMY! WHO CARES THAT MY CITIZENS HATE YOU YANKS?

· MIDSIZE SYRIAN/IRANIAN/ N. KOREAN CITY NAMED FOR YOU
· PREFERRED STATUS FOR OUR NEXT WAR
· 20% SHARE OF OIL PIPELINE TRANSIT FEES

U.S. COLONIAL PROVISIONAL AUTHORITY BUSINESS DEVELOP. DEPT.

Are we looking like looters yet?

Two senior Democratic Congressmen, Henry Waxman and John Dingell, are asking the General Accounting Office to look into these sleazy kickback deals. "These ties between the vice president and Halliburton have raised concerns about whether the company has received favorable treatment from the administration," their letter reads. Well, duh. But don't count on appropriate action—such as impeachment proceedings—from the do-nothing Dems.

Bush's right-wing Gang of Four—Cheney, Rummy, Condi and Wolfy—saw Operation Iraqi Freedom as a chance to line their buddies' pockets, emasculate the Muslim world, place U.S. military bases in Russia's former sphere of influence and, according to the experts, lower the price of oil by busting OPEC. "There will be a substantial increase in Iraqi oil production [under U.S. occupation], and I wouldn't be surprised if schemes emerged to weaken, if not destroy, OPEC," says Jumberto Calderón, former energy minister of Venezuela. Former OPEC Secretary General Fadhil Chalabi (no relation to Ahmed) estimates that increased exploration could potentially double Iraq's proven reserves, which would raise production from 2.4 to 10 million barrels a day. Such Saudi-scale production would "bring OPEC to its knees," says Chalabi. The cartel's member nations, ten of eleven of them predominantly Muslim, would suffer staggering increases in poverty as a result of falling oil revenues, plunging some into the political chaos that breeds Islamist fundamentalism. Meanwhile, the people of Iraq, whose self-flagellating Shias already make the evening news look like a rerun of Iran's 1979 Islamic revolution, would starve as foreign infidels raked in billions, thanks to the oil beneath their land.

Time to dust off your Homeland Security-issued duct tape.

The Fictional War on Terrorism

A wave of bombings left at least 20 people dead in Morocco's busi-
ness capital Casablanca late Friday, the official Map news agency
reported. Three car bombs exploded, near the Belgian consulate, a
Jewish centre and the Hotel Safir. Another bomb went off near the
"Casa de Espana" Hispanic centre, leaving at least 20 people dead,
including two police officers and a security guard, Map reported.
Witnesses said that suicide bombers were involved in the attacks.
—*Agence France-Presse, May 17, 2003*

MAY 20, 2003—We've killed thousands of Muslims and taken over two of their countries. We're spending billions of dollars to make it easier for our government to spy on us. But we haven't caught Osama, al-Qaeda is doing better than ever and airport security is still a sick joke. So when are Americans going to demand a *real* war on terrorism?

Recent suicide bombings in Riyadh and Casablanca proved with bloody eloquence that al-Qaeda and similar extremist groups are anything but "on the run," as George W. Bush puts it. Bush's tactics are a hundred percent failure, yet his band of clueless Christian soldiers continues to go after mosquitoes with shotguns. "So far," Bush spun furiously after the latest round of attacks, "nearly one-half of al-Qaeda's senior operatives have been captured or killed," promising to "remain on the hunt until they are all brought to justice."

Can Bush really be this stupid? Most underground organizations, including al-Qaeda, employ a loose hierarchical structure. No individual member is indispensable, so the capture of even a high-ranking official cannot compromise the group. Each lost member is instantly replaced by the next man down in his cell. It doesn't matter whether we catch half, three-quarters or all of al-Qaeda's leadership—hunting down individual terrorists is an expensive and pointless game of whack-a-mole. Only Allah knows how many eager recruits have sprung up, hydra-like, to fill Khalid Sheikh Mohammad's flip-flops.

Senator and Democratic presidential candidate Bob Graham caught heat for calling the war on Iraq "a distraction" from the war on terrorism, but he was far too kind. The invasions of Afghanistan and Iraq have *replaced* a real war on terrorism, and they've vastly increased the likelihood of future September 11s. Bombing Afghanistan scattered bin Laden, his lieutenants and their foot soldiers everywhere from Chechnya to Sudan to China's Xinjiang province; fleeing Talibs spread new anti-American seed cells while the Taliban and other

radical groups retain their pre-9/11 Pakistani headquarters. With radical Shiite clerics like the Ayatollah Mohammad Baqer al-Hakim poised to fill the post-Saddam power vacuum, Iraq could become a Shia version of Taliban-era Afghanistan: an anarchic collection of fiefdoms run by extremist warlords happy to host training camps for terrorist organizations.

"We're much safer," Tom Ridge claims. If this is safety, gimme danger.

Taking over Iraq and Afghanistan didn't score us any new fans among Muslims. We could have won them over with carefully crafted occupations, but chose instead to allow the two states to disintegrate into chaos and civil war.

Rarely have incompetence and cheapness been wed with such impressively disastrous results. In Afghanistan, we paid off warlords whom we should have dropped bombs upon. Puppet president Hamid Karzai is threatening to abdicate his Kabul city-state because "there is no money in the government treasury."

As *USA Today* reported on May 7, 2003, "Iraqis say they view the U.S. military with suspicion, anger and frustration. Many even say life was in some ways better under the regime of Saddam Hussein: the streets, they say, were safer, jobs more secure, food more plentiful and electricity and water supplies reliable." That's not the message we want on Al Jazeera—whose Baghdad correspondent, in the ultimate case of PR gone awry, U.S. forces killed in Iraq.

"Governance is a long-term process," says Bush Administration reconstruction official Chris Milligan, but that's just another lame excuse. The truth is that we haven't even tried to restore law and order, much less govern. The Pentagon plans to leave just two divisions—30,000 men—to patrol Iraq. That's significantly fewer than the 50,000 peacekeeping troops NATO stationed in Kosovo—a nation less than one-fifth the size of Iraq. Ninety-five percent of Afghanistan has no peacekeepers whatsoever, with fewer than 8,000 in Kabul.

We're sleeping soundly, but the guys who hate us so much they're willing to die to make their point are industriously exploiting our stupidity to sign up new jihadis. "Since the United States invaded Iraq in March," the *Times* quoted top Administration honchos on May 16, "the [al-Qaeda] network has experienced a spike in recruitment."

Ariel Sharon offers living proof that hard-ass tactics strengthen, rather than weaken terrorist groups. Each time Israel assassinates a Palestinian leader or demolishes an Arab home, moderates enraged by those actions become radicalized. Israelis and Palestinians have suffered through this endless attack-retaliation-attack cycle for decades. Surely we can learn from their pain.

It's still early in this game. Shut down the bloated and pointless Homeland Security bureaucracy—since it doesn't include the CIA and FBI it didn't stop interagency squabbling—and apply the money we'll save into a fully funded rebuilding of Iraq and Afghanistan. Charge the Guantánamo detainees with a crime or send them home; their legal limbo is an international embarrassment. Stop fingerprinting Muslim tourists—it's insulting and does nothing to prevent terrorists from entering the country. Quit supporting brutal anti-American military dictators like Pakistan's Pervez Musharraf, whose oppressed subjects rightly blame us for their misery.

"The only way to deal with [terrorists] is to bring them to justice," Bush says. "You can't talk to them, you can't negotiate with them, you must find them." He couldn't be more mistaken. We'll never find them all. And while we shouldn't negotiate with those who call us the Great Satan, we must talk to the millions of Muslims who watch the news every night. Their donations keep al-Qaeda going. If we want them to stop financing the terrorists, we'd better stop acting like a Great Satan.

Slaughtergate

"To suggest that Saddam Hussein threw out the inspectors and therefore used the fact that the inspectors were gone to destroy his weapons is fanciful. It's a fit of imagination. So the fact is he did design a system that was intended to conceal it from the inspectors. After all, even in the early to mid '90s, when we did find the proof of the weapons of mass destruction, it was only after defectors told us about it. The inspectors were in the country, and they were unable to find it because of the great lengths the Saddam Hussein regime had gone to perfect their ability to hide and to conceal. And we still are in an environment where whatever they hid and whatever they concealed could remain hidden and concealed. In addition to the fact, the President said earlier, that they may have destroyed some of it."
—*White House Spokesman Ari Fleischer, June 17, 2003*

JUNE 10, 2003—George W. Bush told us that Iraq and al-Qaeda were working together. They weren't. He repeatedly implied that Iraq had something to do with 9/11. It hadn't. He claimed to have proof that Saddam Hussein possessed banned weapons of mass destruction. He didn't. As our allies watched in horror and disgust, Bush conned us into a one-sided war of aggression that killed and maimed thousands of innocent people, destroyed billions of dollars in Iraqi infrastructure, cost tens of billions of dollars, cost the lives of American soldiers, and transformed our international image as the world's shining beacon of freedom into that of a marauding police state. Presidents Nixon and Clinton rightly faced impeachment for comparatively trivial offenses; if we hope to restore our nation's honor, George W. Bush too must face a president's gravest political sanction.

As the Bush Administration sold Congress and the public on the "threat" posed by Saddam Hussein last winter, White House flack Ari Fleischer assured the American people: "The President of the United States and the Secretary of Defense would not assert as plainly and vocally as they have that Iraq has weapons of mass destruction if it was not true and if they did not have a solid basis for saying it." That's unambiguous rhetoric. But since allied occupation forces have failed to find WMDs, Bush is backtracking: "I am absolutely convinced with time we'll find out that they did have a weapons *program*," the C-in-C says now. What's next? Claiming that Saddam had WMDs because, you know, you could just feel it?

A ferocious power struggle is taking place between Langley and the White House. "It's

hard to tell if there was a breakdown in intelligence or a breakdown in the way intelligence was used," says Michele Flournoy of the Center for Strategic and International Studies. No it's not. Career analysts at the Central and Defense Intelligence Agencies, furious at Bush for sticking them with the blame for the weapons scandal, are leaking prewar memoranda that indicate that the Administration covered up the spooks' assessments, making the case for war with a pile of lies constructed on a bedrock of oil-fueled greed.

A September 2002 DIA study said that there was "no reliable information on whether Iraq is producing and stockpiling chemical weapons," but Bush ignored the report—and told us the exact opposite. After Bush used the discovery of two alleged mobile weapons labs to claim "we found the weapons of mass destruction," CIA "dissenters" shot back that Bush had lied about their reports and that they "doubted the trailers were used to make germ agents, not[ing] that the plants lacked gear for steam sterilization, which is typically necessary for making bioweapons." Defense Secretary Donald Rumsfeld parried: "Any indication or allegation that the intelligence was in any way politicized, of course, is just false on its face...We haven't found Saddam Hussein either, but no one's doubting that he was there."

Both factions are missing the point. Calling for a full Congressional investigation, Sen. Carl Levin (D-MI) of the Armed Services Committee, says: "I think that the nation's credibility is on the line, as well as Bush's."

Assuming that one accepts preemption as a legitimate cause for war—and one ought not—you must possess airtight substantiation that a nation poses an imminent and significant threat before you drop bombs on its cities. Evidence that falls short of hundred percent proof, presented in advance, doesn't pass the pre-empt test.

Bush claimed to have that proof. He said that Iraq could deploy its biological and chem-

ical weapons with just forty-five minutes notice. He painted gruesome pictures of American cities in ruins, their debris irradiated by an Iraqi "dirty bomb." It was all a bald-faced lie, and lying presidents get impeached.

George W. Bush, like Richard Nixon, "endeavor[ed] to misuse the Central Intelligence Agency." George W. Bush, like Richard Nixon, "[made] or caus[ed] to be made false or misleading public statements for the purpose of deceiving the people of the United States." (The legalese comes from the first Article of Impeachment against Nixon, passed by the House Judiciary Committee on July 27, 1974. Faced with certain impeachment in the House and conviction in the Senate, Nixon resigned two weeks later.) In the words of Bill Clinton's 1998 impeachment, George W. Bush "has undermined the integrity of his office, has brought disrepute on the Presidency, has betrayed his trust as President, and has acted in a manner subversive of the rule of law and justice, to the manifest injury of the people of the United States."

Nixon and Clinton escaped criminal prosecution for burglary, perjury and obstruction of justice. George W. Bush, however, stands accused as the greatest mass murderer in American history. The Lexington Institute estimates that the U.S. killed between 15,000 and 20,000 Iraqi troops during the fraudulently justified invasion of Iraq; more than 150 U.S. soldiers died. A new Associated Press study of Iraqi civilian casualties reports at least 3,240 dead.

Although Bush, Rumsfeld, Colin Powell and Condoleeza Rice denied such legal niceties to the concentration-camp inmates captured in their illegal invasions of Iraq and Afghanistan, these high-ranking Administration henchmen should be quickly turned over—after impeachment proceedings for what might properly be called Slaughtergate—to an international tribunal for prosecution for war crimes.

Anything less would be anti-American.

Bush's Willing Executioners

Grassroots Democratic activists believe America is in desperate trouble. At the recent Take Back America conference in Washington, which brought together the core of the party's liberal wing and the politicians who wanted to win its support, there was a conviction that George Bush is more than simply a bad president, an heir to Reagan or Nixon. He is the worst president ever, a leader so destructive to all that progressives value that the damage from his reign may be irrevocable. For liberals, Bush is a national emergency.

Yet to the country at large, Bush appears to remain an affable fellow and resolute leader. A CNN/USA Today/Gallup Poll taken last week shows that 67 percent of Americans believe the administration has not deliberately misled the public about Iraq's weapons, despite much reporting to the contrary. A recent Fox News poll indicates that most respondents said Bush's tax cuts won't help their families, but, astonishingly, the same poll shows that 47 percent think the cuts are a good idea, compared to 44 percent who think they're not. In the latest Ipsos-Reid/Cook Political Report Poll, the president's approval ratings were 61 percent.

The question is whether Democrats can make their anger work for them and communicate it outside their own confabs. After all, rage is a tricky thing in politics. It fuels the shock troops of the right wing, but it also can blow up in their faces (see Bob Barr and Newt Gingrich). For Democrats, it could galvanize an untapped resentment of Bush—or leave them marginalized by a media eager to parrot Republican attacks.

—Michelle Goldberg, Salon, June 11, 2003

JUNE 17, 2003—Today's version of the heroic Nathan Hale would fall to his knees, beg for mercy, and swear fealty to the British crown. A 21st century Patrick Henry would no doubt argue that homeland security trumps personal liberty. Benedict Arnold would make the rounds of the TV talk shows, lauded as a "heroic pragmatist." In a land of wimps, the dimwit is king—such is the dismal state of post-9/11 America.

As George W. Bush's aristocorporate junta runs roughshod over hard-earned free-

doms, as his lunatic-right Administration loots $10 trillion from the national treasury, as his armies invade sovereign nations without cause, as he threatens war against imagined enemies while allowing real ones to build nuclear weapons, those charged with standing against these perversions of American values remain appallingly, inexplicably silent.

We have become a nation of cowards, and I am ashamed.

Where are the Democrats? Under our two-party system it is their patriotic duty to represent the opinions and beliefs of their constituents, who are mostly liberal. That responsibility becomes an urgent necessity when the GOP, in firm control of all three branches of government, abandons a proud tradition of conservatism in favor of outright fascism. With the exception of a few principled men like Senator Robert Byrd (D-WV), leading Democrats have made little or no effort to stymie Bush's agenda, launch a real investigation of 9/11 or appoint a special prosecutor to go after the WMD scandal. To their eternal dishonor, eighty-two Democratic Congressmen and twenty-nine Senators voted for the invasion of Iraq—this despite the pleas of millions of demonstrators. Among the nine leading contenders for the Democratic presidential nomination, only two have made opposition to runaway militarism a staple of their stump speech.

Easily spooked and even more easily fooled, Democratic leaders are neither leading nor acting like Democrats. Thirty years of political duck-and-cover have brought them to the brink of irrelevance. Far more damning, they have abandoned their rightful role as loyal opponents.

Where is the left? The radical theoreticians who provided the intellectual rationale for opposition to the Vietnam War—Ralph Nader, Noam Chomsky, et al—are touring the nation's universities, each pushing books and promoting their personal "brand" to youthful idealists. Former leftist Christopher Hitchens, who so desperately wanted to fit into the new Republican paradigm that he endorsed attacking Iraq, has been reduced to insisting that weapons of mass destruction will turn up someday. Probably.

Unlike Saddam, Bush needn't cut out his opponents' tongues. They're keeping silent on their own.

It may be naïve to pose the question, but where are the principled Republicans? Not long ago, conservative leaders trudged down from Capitol Hill to tell an embattled Richard Nixon that he could no longer count on their support. Now the moderate, fiscally responsible Republicans one might expect to stand up to Bush's fiscal depredations— men like John McCain, Bob Dole and George Pataki—remain mute as their party and nation are hijacked by fanatics. Bush's rich man's welfare will cost the average U.S. citizen

$500,000 over the next decade—isn't that the kind of government waste Republicans are supposed to deplore?

Partisan politics are so dead that the American resistance is entrusted by default to the unlikely hands of the same intelligence establishment that poisoned Fidel's cigars. Every day brings startling revelations from pissed-off CIA and Defense Intelligence Agency spymasters: despite what Bush said over and over, there was never any proof that Iraq had weapons of mass destruction, the trailers Bush claimed were mobile chemical weapons labs were no such thing, and Colin Powell presented, in the U.N., evidence on Iraq that he privately considered doctored and unreliable. The recent DIA leak of a November 2002 analysis shows that intelligence experts believed that Saddam Hussein would never use WMDs—even if he had them—unless "regime survival was imminently threatened." The Iraqis would use them only "in extreme circumstances," the report said, "because their use would confirm Iraq's evasion of U.N. restrictions."

Where is the outrage? Even though it's painfully clear that Bush lied about the WMDs, even though daily ambushes of American troops indicate that the war is far from over, a CBS News poll shows that 62 percent of Americans still support Bush's con job on Iraq. "The president is ninety-nine percent safe on this one," says Newt Gingrich.

Protestors who demonstrated against the war before it began ought to be energized by the WMD scandal, but the streets of Washington are quiet. Editors who parroted the Administration's lies, given the chance to redeem themselves now, downplay the latest Slaughtergate news. An army colonel e-mails, urging me to keep asking questions, yet confesses, "I'm keeping my thoughts to myself and waiting until I retire to get the hell out of here." Daniel Goldhagen's controversial 1996 book *Hitler's Willing Executioners: Ordinary Germans and the Holocaust* pointed out an obvious truth: that the Nazis could never have triumphed, retained power or gotten anything done without the explicit complicity of the people they ruled. Therefore, Goldhagen argued—and thoughtful people agree—the failure of the German people to resist Hitler made them just as guilty as he was.

How will history judge us?

A Crack in Bush's Façade

*Senator Robert Bennett (R-Utah) defended the Bush administra-
tion's decision to confront Iraq over its weapons of mass destruction
in a speech to the Senate June 5. [He] noted that the United States
has yet to find Saddam Hussein. "Does that mean he never existed or he was never in Iraq?" he asked, "Of course not. The same
thing applies to the weapons of mass destruction," Bennett said.*
—Steve LaRoque, Washington File, June 5, 2003

JUNE 24, 2003—Bush lied about the weapons of mass destruction. He lied to us, the United
Nations, and the soldiers he sent to die in Iraq. Bush's apologists defend his attempts to sell
his obscene war as mere spin, but claiming certain knowledge of something that doesn't exist
is hardly a question of emphasis. It's time to stop wondering where the WMDs are. Even if
nukes and gases and anthrax turn up in prodigious quantities, it won't matter. Proof of Bush's
perfidy, unlike his accusations that Saddam had something to do with 9/11, is already
irrefutable.

Before he ordered U.S. forces to kill and maim tens of thousands of innocent Iraqi soldiers and civilians, Bush and Co. repeatedly maintained that they possessed absolute proof
that Saddam Hussein still possessed WMDs. "There is no doubt that Saddam Hussein now
has weapons of mass destruction," Dick Cheney said in August.

WMDs -not a "WMD program" as they now refer to it.

WMDs -not just indications of possible, or probable, WMDs.

Absolute proof.

During the first days of the war, Defense Secretary Donald Rumsfeld stared into television cameras and said that he knew exactly where they were. "We know where they are,"
Rumsfeld said. "They are in the area around Tikrit and Baghdad."

Uh-huh. So where are they?

"Absolute" proof is a high standard—heck, it's a nearly impossible benchmark. The last
time I checked, my cat was in my kitchen, licking the milk at the bottom of my cereal bowl.
As intel goes, mine is triple-A-rated—I witnessed it this morning, and I've spent the better
part of a decade observing that animal's habits. But if you were to demand absolute proof of
kitty's current location, I couldn't give it to you. I'd bet that he's sleeping on my bed. But he
could be in the litter box or on the windowsill. Truth is, I don't know where he is. To say otherwise, to present even a well-founded hypothesis as Fact, would be a lie.

Bush had conjecture, wishful thinking and stale intelligence going for him. He needed

absolute proof, and the absence thereof is leading to talk of impeachment. Before the invasion of Iraq, Rumsfeld argues, "Virtually everyone agreed they did [have WMDs] in Congress, in successive Democratic and Republican administrations, in the intelligence communities here in the United States, and also in foreign countries and at the U.N., even among those countries that did not favor military action in Iraq." Untrue.

Most people, me included, guessed that Iraq *probably* had WMDs. (Those of us who opposed the war figured that Iraq's post-Gulf War partitioning, trade sanctions and maximum 400-mile missile range limited its potential threat to the United States.) The last time we knew for sure that Iraq had WMDs was 1998. The American public, nervous about Bush's radical new policy of preemptive warfare, would not have supported a war based on maybes. In September 2002 only 18 percent of Americans thought attacking Saddam would make America safer.

The Bush Administration didn't have proof, so they spent last fall making it up. As Robin Cook, who resigned from Tony Blair's cabinet over the war, told the British Parliament, "Instead of using intelligence as evidence on which to base a decision about policy, we used intelligence as the basis to justify a policy on which we had already decided."

By January 2003, 81 percent of respondents to an ABC News poll said they believed that Iraq "posed a threat to the United States."

Previous administrations, reliant on the CIA for reliable information, have traditionally respected a "Chinese wall" between Langley and the White House. As Republicans blame the CIA for the missing WMDs, leaks from within the CIA increasingly indicate that Dick Cheney and others sought to politicize its reports on Iraq, cherry-picking factoids that backed its war cry and dismissing those that didn't. This dubious practice culminated in

Colin Powell's over-the-top performance before the U.N., where he misrepresented documents he knew to be forged—which he privately derided as "bullshit"!—as hard fact.

The Administration's defenders, whose selective morality makes Bill Clinton look like a saint, argue that the WMDs don't matter, that Saddam's mass graves vindicate the war liars. But no one denied that Hussein was evil. The American people knew that Saddam was a butcher during the '80s when we backed him, and during the '90s when we contained him. They weren't willing to go to war over regime change in the '00s, which is why the Administration invented a fictional threat.

Lying to the American people is impeachable. But insiders have to talk before the media can aggressively pursue the WMD story, prosecutors can be appointed and top evildoers brought to justice. Finally, Slaughtergate has its own Alexander Butterfield. Christian Westermann, a respected State Department intelligence analyst talking to Congress, has testified that Undersecretary of State John Bolton, a Bush political appointee, pressured him to change a report on Cuba so that it would back Bush claims that Cuba was developing biological weapons. Westermann says that when he refused, Bolton tried to have him transferred.

Westermann's testimony doesn't relate to Iraq, but it puts the lie to Bushoid assertions that they never messed with the CIA. A reliable source informs me that there's a "jihad" underway between Administration political operatives and the career intelligence community. "Guys are pissed off that they're being asked to take the fall for the White House. Look for more leaks in the future," this official says.

Meanwhile, General Richard Meyers, chairman of the Joint Chiefs of Staff, has been reduced to parsing the meaning of intelligence: "Intelligence doesn't necessarily mean something is true," he says.

Now he tells us.

Bush's Cover-Up Precedes the Scandal

Mr. Bush is at the centre of a political storm over a 16-word pas-sage in his State of the Union speech in January in which he said the British government had learned that Saddam had been trying to acquire uranium from Niger. George Tenet, the CIA director, has taken the blame for the Niger claim but there have been alle-gations his staff were under pressure from White House aides to agree to its inclusion in the speech even though the agency was very doubtful about its truth.

With American soldiers being killed in Iraq nearly every day, Mr. Bush is facing a political backlash and attention is being focused on whether intelligence was manipulated.
—Toby Harnden, UK Telegraph, July 21, 2003

JULY 21, 2003—"When it's all said and done," Bush still confidently insists, "the people of the United States and the world will realize that Saddam Hussein had a weapons program." This once again begs the question of presidential dyslexia: You're supposed to find the WMDs *before* the war of preemption, silly rabbit!

This bizarro Administration does everything bass-ackwards. The recession is hardest on the poor and middle-class, so Bush gives tax cuts to the rich. When an overwhelming inva-sion force was needed to secure Afghanistan and Iraq, Rumsfeld sent in a skeleton crew. Now that the citizens of those countries want us to go home, General Tommy Franks has announced that our 148,000-man, $5 billion-a-month occupation army will get bigger and stick around until whenever.

Now the Bushists are reversing the traditional lifecycle of every political ruckus from Teapot Dome to Watergate. Knowing that most scandals last as long as a mosquito, smart politicians wait to see whether a given outrage will spark lasting popular fury before con-cocting a risky cover-up. Not these guys. They've started the cover-up before the scandal has had a chance to catch on.

Little things hook big fish: tax evasion for Al Capone, a minor stock trade for Martha Stewart, a sexual dalliance for Bill Clinton. So it is with George W. Bush: whether or not the man who conned us into two wars ends up sharing a cage with Khalid Sheikh Mohammad could come down to this line from the 2003 State of the Union address: "The British government has learned that Saddam Hussein recently sought significant quantities of uranium from Africa."

The source for that claim is a now-debunked British intelligence dossier from September 24, 2002. Forged letters in the UK report purport to document Iraq's attempts to purchase 550 tons of "yellowcake" uranium ore from Niger. No one is saying who forged the fake purchase orders, though Foreign Secretary Jack Straw claims that the "dodgy dossier" came from a third, unknown, nation.

"A bunch of bull," Ari Fleischer calls the simmering scandal, ridiculing the suggestion that fear of Iraqi nukes was "why we went to war, a central issue of why we went to war."

In fact, in the same State of the Union address in which he referenced Niger, Bush did make Iraqi nuclear weapons a "central issue." "Imagine those nineteen hijackers with other weapons and other plans—this time armed by Saddam Hussein," Bush leered into the cameras. "It would take one vial, one canister, one crate slipped into this country to bring a day of horror like none we have ever known." Vials, canisters and crates refer to, respectively, biological, chemical and nuclear weapons.

Almost immediately after receiving it from the British, CIA analysts determined that the Niger info was probably bogus. According to the *New York Times,* CIA director George Tenet next personally met with Deputy National Security Adviser Stephen Hadley—Condi Rice's right-hand man—to make sure Bush didn't mention Niger uranium ore anymore. The UN's International Atomic Energy Agency went further, determining that Iraq simply didn't have a nuke program. Based on these facts, "The reference was omitted when Mr. Bush gave [a] speech in Cincinnati on October 7." And it stayed out of Bush's talks until it suddenly popped up in the State of the Union—despite more CIA warnings. Even then, Secretary of State Colin Powell refused to use it in his presentation to the U.N. a week later. "It was not standing the test of time," admits a squeamish Powell.

Behold the smoking gun: Not only had the CIA told the White House about the Niger forgery in October 2002, the White House had gotten the message. Nonetheless Bush, after months of excising that argument from his speeches, revived it in January 2003 for use in what is historically the most widely watched TV appearance a president makes each year.

Many Americans knew that Bush was lying about Iraqi WMDs. They just didn't care, which is how he retains a 59 percent job approval rating. After getting called on his lies, a smarter politician would have apologized and said that liberating Iraq justified a few fibs.

Considering the conventional wisdom that Bush's idiocy is mitigated by his brilliant cabinet, Bush opted for a weird defense: I'm not a liar—my staff is incompetent! And so the cover-up began.

In the most transparently brokered deal since Ford's pardon of Nixon, Tenet agreed to take the blame for the Niger imbroglio in exchange for not taking the fall. "These sixteen words should never have been included in the text written for the president," said Tenet in a prepared statement. "The president is pleased that the director of Central Intelligence acknowledged what needed to be acknowledged," said Ari Fleischer the next day. Bush got his patsy and Tenet kept his job. But career CIA staffers are furious at Bush for sticking them with the blame for a snafu they specifically tried to talk him out of. This scandal is just beginning.

Lying about Niger yellowcake pales next to Bush's other evil chicanery: hobbling the U.S. economy with debt, feeding corporate corruption, opening concentration camps for Muslims and bombing thousands of people to death. But those acts are almost too monstrous to comprehend. Americans easily understand the myriad of little lies—the faked Jessica Lynch "rescue," the phony Saddam statue toppling and now the Niger uranium story—and how they add up to the character of a man unworthy of the office he holds.

Liberation of the Unwilling

President Bush has ordered the Pentagon to deploy American troops off the coast of Liberia to support a West African peacekeeping force that is expected to arrive in the embattled country within two weeks.

The president did not clarify how many American troops would be deployed, for how long, or what their exact role will be, except to say that the number of soldiers would be "limited" and that the American "commitment is to enable ECOWAS to go in," referring to the Economic Community of West African States, which will oversee the deployment of the West African peacekeepers. Earlier, in a written statement announcing the American deployment, the chief White House spokesman, Scott McClellan, said, "The U.S. role will be limited in time and scope."

The announcement came during a day of intense bombardment in the center of Monrovia, Liberia's capital, which is under siege by rebels opposed to the government of President Charles Taylor. Mortar bombs slammed into a compound owned by the American Embassy, killing at least 12 Liberians and wounding more than 100, according to news agency reports.

—Kirk Semple, New York Times, July 25, 2003

JULY 25, 2003—"If war is forced upon us," Bush once proclaimed, "we will liberate the people of Iraq from a cruel and violent dictator." Now Liberia, a nation founded by former American slaves and whose Constitution, flag, language and civil administration are modeled on those of the United States, is deteriorating as a bloody civil war devolves into total anarchy. Close to a thousand civilians have died, caught in the crossfire between government and rebel forces, during the last few days alone. Here is Bush's stirring message of hope for the miserable people of Liberia: "We continue to monitor the situation very closely."

First we attacked Iraq, which posed no threat, while ignoring North Korea, which did. Taking a stance which defies common decency and common sense, we're now stiff-arming people who are literally dying for our help—while forcing ourselves on others who are willing to die to avoid our presence. Apparently, whether or not Bush "liberates" you has nothing to do with how badly your country needs liberation.

Last fall, government and talk-radio loudmouths claimed that they had the power to

read the hearts and minds of Iraq's 25,000,000 citizens. Now the results of their intelligence failure are in: Iraqis prefer Saddam's homegrown autocracy to our 148,000 infidel storm troopers. They're voting with mines, rocket-propelled grenades and AK-47s in ambushes so frequent that the media doesn't bother to report them until someone gets killed. Graffiti cover the walls of Iraqi cities: "Pray for Saddam's victory because he's a genuine Iraqi." "May the occupation fall and may Saddam return."

The resistance owns the highways, the alleys and the nights, forcing hapless American forces to scurry in convoys between their cantonments. On average they kill one of our soldiers every day—152 so far—and cripple another half-dozen. Iraqi collaborators are executed nightly. They're sending a clear message to the American people: get your Kevlar-coated goons out. Sunni *imams* in Fallujah, the *Los Angeles Times* reported on July 15, rejected food from soldiers of the Third Infantry Division. "We would rather eat rocks than eat chickens from Americans," one cleric said. "Even the poorest person in Fallujah doesn't want chickens from you." Children threw rocks at the U.S. soldiers as they retreated with their proffered poultry.

We haven't lost as many young men and women in Afghanistan, but that's because fewer are there to begin with: a mere 10,000, most of whom are holed up at Kabul's Bagram air base. Before the October 2001 invasion, Bush decided against posting peacekeepers in the ninety-five percent of the country that needed them; now Afghanistan belongs to warlords and their tribal militias. And we're not winning popularity contests even in the rump city-state of Kabul. Hamid Karzai's puppet regime is broke, and the tiny amount of U.S. aid went entirely to non-government organizations which spent it on SUVs and fancy offices. Nothing substantial has been rebuilt for ordinary Afghans. "N.G.O.," spat an unpaid Kabul

cop at the *New York Times'* Khaled Hosseini. "What have they done for us? I have yet to see them put two bricks together."

Twenty peacekeepers have been killed so far in Afghanistan, meaning that that assignment offers roughly the same 1-in-400 odds of dying as a one-year tour of duty in Iraq.

Regime change in Liberia, on the other hand, would be a cakewalk. Unlike Iraq and Afghanistan, the country has a strong historical connection with us—streets and airports are named after U.S. presidents, and the American dollar is the national currency. Liberian strongman Charles Taylor has promised to go into Nigerian exile. Crowds have rioted in Monrovia in *favor* of U.S. intervention. Taylor's only demand is that we show up to avoid a power vacuum after he steps down, but Bush—who hasn't learned from the chaos in Baghdad—has refused.

Considering recent history, sending in the Marines would also be the right thing to do. President Reagan and Bush's father funded a military coup in 1980 that led to Taylor's 1989 seizure of power and a seven-year-long civil war that killed more than 200,000 people. American taxpayers funded that carnage; they should now help end it.

The trouble is, Liberia doesn't fit into Bush-Cheney's policy of "total energy dominance." That's why a White House determined to invade Iran during its second term has only dispatched a few dozen soldiers to guard the U.S. embassy. While neighboring countries have an estimated 60 billion barrels of oil in all, Liberia itself possesses insignificant reserves. Iraq, on the other hand, is the world's second largest oil-producing state. And the U.S. invaded Afghanistan principally as a conduit to the oil- and gas-rich Caspian Sea.

Hopefully Bush will cave in to public pressure by transferring a significant troop complement from Iraq and Afghanistan to Liberia. Until then, Liberia's best hope is striking oil.

Bring Home the Troops

U.S. occupation forces said they had killed 11 resistance fighters, who attempted to ambush a patrol north of Baghdad on Friday. Earlier in the day, the military said that a sniper shot dead a U.S. soldier guarding the national museum in Baghdad overnight. Another 19 were wounded when they came under fire near the town of Balad, north of the capital. Another soldier was wounded on Friday by a blast targeting a Humvee vehicle on the outskirts of Baghdad, witnesses said.

At least 10 U.S. soldiers were wounded and three Iraqis killed in four incidents in Iraq on Thursday, a day after U.S. President George W. Bush defiantly vowed that resistance attacks would not drive out American troops. Resistance fighters have stepped up military operations in recent weeks. Attacks launched against occupation forces have become a daily occurrence.

—Al Jazeera Television, July 4, 2003

JULY 29, 2003—There's only one way the war against Iraq could have gone worse: if Bush hadn't been lying about Saddam's nuclear program. But short of a Manhattan mushroom cloud, it's hard to imagine a darker scenario than the one we're in. No WMDs. No Saddam. Millions of new enemies. Billions in new debt. And an estimated 35,000 guerrillas exacting a terrible tithe—one dead American soldier for every day we stay where we don't belong.

For the cameras, military and Bush Administration officials keep putting a brave face on their folly-turned-quagmire-turned-debacle. Hey, that's their job. The most recent "bring 'em on" moment comes courtesy of General Richard Meyers, chairman of the Joint Chiefs of Staff. Meyers assures us that the President of Iraq's bloodied mug will soon join those of his sons broadcast on Death TV, and that such appearances will reduce attacks on U.S. forces: "If [Saddam is] still alive, it's just a matter of time. He is so busy saving his own skin, he is having no impact, no impact on the security situation."

A day after Meyers's rosy prediction, Iraqi resistance fighters bombed an American Humvee in central Baghdad, killing one U.S. soldier and wounding three others.

Paul Wolfowitz was certain the Iraqi people, eager for liberation, would throw roses at our troops. Cakewalk city, promised Cheney. Major combat is over, Bush announced at his thumbs-up aircraft carrier photo op. We'll only need to stay a few months, swore Tommy Franks. We know exactly where the WMDs are, insisted Rumsfeld. We've found the

WMDs, said Bush. Well, we will find them, they all say, though not often anymore. Every single thing they tell us turns out to be dead wrong.

Now they say things are getting better. Read the paper. Watch the tube. E-mail a soldier stationed in Iraq. Does the occupation of Iraq seem to you like it's getting better?

We've got 148,000 occupation soldiers sweating out summer days hotter than most Americans will ever experience in their lifetimes. Facing a minimum two-to-four-year occupation timetable, the Pentagon won't say if or when those guys will come home to their relatives, some of whom are so frustrated that they've formed the group Military Families Speak Out to demand the return of their loved ones. At the present rate of carnage, an American soldier's chances of coming home in a bag are 1 in 400, and nobody knows how many Iraqis are dying. Pundits compare this to Vietnam, but that's unfair. It took years for LBJ to screw up Vietnam this badly.

It's time to stop throwing good lives after bad. We came for Iraq's oil, but we'll never extract crude without seducing Iraqi hearts and minds. That war was lost before we fired the first Cruise missiles in March, for a few simple reasons. First, Iraqis spent the '90s dodging American bombs and trade sanctions. We never knew their pain; they'll never forget it. Second, our invasion allowed looters and rapists to take over the cities. Anyone who is short a car or a daughter rightly blames us for their loss. Third, we've transformed one of the Arab world's few semi-modern secular states into an anarchic Third World dump. Iraqis hate us. They trust us to do the wrong thing each and every time.

Central Command has issued a directive to U.S. forces: When a car approaches your checkpoint, fire "warning" shots at its engine. If it doesn't stop, kill everyone inside. This policy results in a lot of dead, unarmed, Iraqi civilians accustomed to standard roadblock protocol (whereby motorists pull up and present ID to police). Some drivers don't hear the bullets pinging off their engine blocks; others assume they're being ambushed by bandits and floor it. Either way, they die. This happens all over the country, yet it never occurs to the geniuses at CentCom to issue new orders. On July 28, U.S. Task Force 20 murdered five innocent Iraqi drivers in Baghdad's Mansur section in this way. "All of the soldiers shot immediately," says Abu Hassan, a local store owner. "The people are angry and very upset."

This isn't going to get better. We're stupid and mean occupiers, which only makes the Iraqis' seething resentment over our inability to restore water and electricity worse. The attacks will continue, as will our inept attempts to quell dissent. Iraq will devolve into an Israel/Palestine-style spiral of attack, retaliation, retaliation, rinse, lather, repeat.

Pro-war or anti-war, most Americans think we're obligated to stick around until we've rebuilt Iraq. Get real! You have only to look at Afghanistan -not that you'll see it on TV- to see that we're never going to build schools, skyscrapers and superhighways in Iraq. Sooner or later, after the American public has quit caring and stopped paying attention and gotten sick of losing a soldier a day, we will withdraw. And when—not if—that happens, Iraq won't be any closer to democracy than it is today.

Why not admit that the invasion was a mistake now, before more people die in a meaningless war? Cut bait and bring home the troops. Sure, the French will mock us; we deserve it. Iraq may become a Shiite theocracy, but nothing—except a brand-new president with a new take on foreign policy—can stop that now. Disaster is inevitable.

It's infinitely better to take a few PR lumps in the international community than to keep feeding the *fedayeen* a fresh-faced youngster every day. Please, Mr. Bush: Bring the troops home.

Time to Get Real in Iraq

The U.N. special representative in Iraq and at least 16 others died Tuesday in a bomb explosion that ripped through the organization's headquarters in Baghdad. Sergio Vieira de Mello, a veteran U.N. official appointed to the post in May, was killed when a bomb-laden cement truck exploded beneath the window of his office in the Canal Hotel at about 4:30 p.m. He was trapped in the rubble for several hours before he died. At least 100 people were wounded.

A U.N. official in New York said Tuesday night that a "substantial" number of bodies remained in the wreckage. Many were burned beyond recognition, and DNA tests will be required to identify them, the official said. Over the weekend, oil, water and electricity lines were attacked by what a coalition spokesman said were saboteurs. Two weeks ago, a car bomb outside the Jordanian Embassy in Baghdad killed 10 people.

—CNN, August 20, 2003

AUGUST 26, 2003—Nearly 70 percent of Americans tell *Newsweek* that "the United States will be bogged down in [Iraq] for years without achieving its goals." Yet 61 percent tell the same poll that invading Iraq was the right thing to do. The reason for this weird disconnect: people think that we're in Iraq to spread democracy and rebuild the Middle East. They think we're The Good Guys. But the longer we keep patting ourselves on the back, the more we tell ourselves that the Iraqi resistance is a bunch of evil freedom-haters, the deeper we'll sink into this quagmire.

It's time to get real.

In war, the side that most accurately sizes up the situation ultimately prevails. In this war in Iraq, our leaders thought the fall of Baghdad meant the end of the conflict. "Mission Accomplished," as the banner behind George W. Bush read on the aircraft carrier. But Saddam understood the truth: the war began with the occupation. Guerrilla warfare offered the only way for Iraq's tiny, poorly armed military to resist the U.S. The Baath Party planned to provoke U.S. occupation forces into mistreating the population.

It worked.

Random bombings and sniper hits have made the American occupiers jittery and paranoid. They've withdrawn into fortified cantonments where they've cut off contact with civil-

ians. Their ignorance causes them to offend Iraqi cultural and religious sensibilities. Even better from Saddam's perspective, U.S. troops push people around: shooting unarmed motorists, stealing their money and jewelry at roadblocks, breaking into houses in the middle of the night, manhandling wives and daughters, putting bags over men's heads and carrying them off to God knows where for who knows how long.

"U.S. troops put their boots on the back of men's heads as they lie face down, forcing their foreheads to the ground," the Associated Press's Scheherezade Faramarzi writes about the procedure used by U.S. troops during sweeps. "There is no greater humiliation...because Islam forbids putting the forehead on the ground except in prayer." In Iraq, we are the bad guys.

What about the "terrorists" who bombed the U.N. headquarters and Jordanian embassy in Baghdad, who sabotage oil and water pipelines, who use rifles and rocket-propelled grenades and remote-controlled mines to kill our soldiers? Aren't these "killers" evil, "killing people who just want to help," as another AP writer puts it? In short: no.

The ad hoc Iraqi resistance is comprised of indigenous fighters ranging from secular ex-Republican Guards to radical Islamist Shiites, as well as foreign Arab volunteers waging the same brand of come-one-come-all jihad that the *mujahedeen* fought against Soviet occupation forces in Afghanistan. While one can dismiss foreign jihadis as naïve adventurers, honest Americans should call native Iraqi resistance fighters by a more fitting name: Iraqi patriots.

One of my favorite propaganda posters from World War II depicts a strapping young SS officer holding a smiling local kid in his arms. "Trust the German soldier," the caption exhorts citizens of occupied France. But when liberation came in 1945, Frenchmen who had obeyed that poster were shot as collaborators. The men and women who resisted—the "ter-

rorists" who shot German soldiers, cut phone lines and bombed trains—later received medals and pensions. Invaders always say that they come as liberators, but it's almost never true.

"We want deeds, not words," says Abu Mohammad, a retired teacher, about our inability (unwillingness?) to restore basic services to the city of Baghdad. Here are our deeds: Talking about democracy as we cancel elections. Guarding the oil ministry building while museums are sacked. Exporting Iraqi oil to Turkey as Iraqis suffer fuel and power shortages. Iraq's natural resources are being raped. Its people are being murdered. Yet it's the patriotic Iraqi resistance, which is trying to stop these outrages by throwing out the perpetrators of an illegal war of aggression, that the Bush Administration dares call "terrorists."

On July 5 a bomb killed seven recruits for a U.S.-trained Iraqi police force in Ramadi. U.S. occupation administrator Paul Bremer deplored the murder of "innocent Iraqis." Cops who work for a foreign army of occupation are not innocent. They are collaborators. Traitors. They had it coming.

Under George W. Bush, truth and justice are no longer the American way. The U.S. occupation of Iraq is misguided, evil and doomed to failure. The sooner we accept this difficult truth, the sooner we decide to stop being the bad guys, the sooner we'll withdraw our troops. The bloodshed may continue after we leave—and we'll be partly to blame for that. But until we pull out, the carnage is *all* ours.

Sami Tuma's brother was shot to death when he drove past a U.S. military checkpoint. "It is simple," says Tuma. "If someone kills your son, wife or brother without any reason but only that they happen to be walking or driving in the street, what will you do? You retaliate."

It's what I'd do. It's probably what you'd do too.

Iraq: What Went Wrong

About 400,000 mourners took to the streets of Najaf Tuesday, flailing their backs and pounding their chests in anguish at the funeral of a leading Shiite cleric assassinated in a car bomb attack. Men clad in white robes and dark uniforms brandishing Kalashnikov rifles stood guard along the roof of the gold-domed Imam Ali mosque, where Ayatollah Mohammed Baqir al-Hakim was killed Friday in the bloodiest attack since the fall of Saddam Hussein. Accounts of the death toll ranged from more than 80 to more than 120. In an angry funeral oration, the cleric's brother blamed the U.S. occupation forces for the lax security that led to the attack at Iraq's most sacred Shiite mosque. He raged against the American troops and demanded they leave Iraq. "The occupation force is primarily responsible for the pure blood that was spilled in holy Al-Najaf," said Abdel-Aziz al-Hakim, the ayatollah's brother and a member of the U.S.-picked Governing Council.

Associated Press, September 2, 2003

SEPTEMBER 2, 2003—In my March 25, 2003 column, I wrote that Bush could salvage a war based on lies only if he played the earnest liberator rather than the crusading colonizer. He had already abandoned Afghanistan; few cared or noticed. But Iraq wasn't nearly as remote. The world would be watching, and we would only have one chance to make a good first impression.

If we were really Iraq's saviors, we should have kept our paws off Iraq's oil reserves, respected Saddam Hussein's oil deals with France, Germany and Russia, and foresworn sweetheart contracts with politically connected corporations. The Pentagon should have inserted enough troops to prevent a civil war, held elections and, most importantly, rebuilt the country's ravaged infrastructure. "It's going to take billions of dollars and several hundred thousand troops at least a decade to get Iraq back on its feet," I predicted, guessing that Bush would create another Vietnam rather than make that investment.

I wish I could pick stocks as accurately.

The bombing of Najaf's Imam Ali mosque, killing pro-U.S. Ayatollah Mohammed Bakr al Hakim and at least ninety of the Shiite faithful, marks the start of full-fledged religious warfare in the U.S.-occupied central and southern sectors. (Our recent *de facto* recognition of a future Kurdistan has effectively ended the prospect of a unified Iraq.) Possible suspects

include fellow Shiite cleric Mukhtader al Sadr, an Iraqi nationalist opposed to the U.S. occupation, Iranian intelligence agents and Sunnis affiliated with Saddam Hussein's deposed government.

Saddam kept Iraq's federation of conflicting tribes and religions together through intimidation and bribery. The Pentagon doesn't have enough troops to accomplish the former and none of the cash needed for the latter, making the old tyrant look great by comparison—and sparking paranoia in the Muslim media. "The Zionists want to divide Iraq into three separate states, a Shiite, a Sunni and a Kurdish state," posits Charles Ayoub in Beirut's *Ad-Diyar* newspaper. "The United States is ruled by the Zionists. The...announcement by U.S. authorities in Iraq that the perpetrators of the [Najaf bombing] belonged to the Sunni Muslim community and to the al-Qaeda organization was aimed at triggering such strife between the Sunnis and Shiites."

Even if we had proved ourselves to be the most benevolent occupiers to ever march through their streets, Iraqis would still have yearned to have their nation back to themselves. We've been anything but.

Our early emphasis on seizing oil fields, and schemes to funnel revenue from the U.N. oil-for-food program into lucrative contracts with Halliburton (which still pays Dick Cheney a huge salary) and MCI-WorldCom (a major Bush-Cheney campaign donor) belie our stated commitment to liberation and spreading democracy. We're more Attila the Hun than Dwight Eisenhower.

Bush, a former businessman, is treating "liberated" Iraq like the victim of a hostile leveraged buy-out. In an LBO, you borrow a target company's purchase price and saddle its balance sheet with the resulting debt, leading to layoffs and possible bankruptcy. In Iraq Bush hopes to defray rising costs of occupation—$1 billion a week for the Pentagon, plus $30 billion to fix water, electricity and oil production facilities—by selling Iraq's oil.

But it's Iraq's oil, not ours.

Asking Iraqis to pay the cost of their own invasion and occupation is outrageous. If we want to waste a billion bucks a week to piss off the Arab world, that's our problem.

Our soldiers disposed of Saddam's army, but they haven't been nearly as effective as good will ambassadors. Partly because they don't speak Arabic or understand Islamic culture, jumpy U.S. soldiers are killing so many Iraqi civilians that the Pentagon is deliberately refusing to keep track of accidental casualties.

The good news, such as it is, is that Bush's neo-con wolf pack is finally beginning to admit that the facts didn't fit with all their bluster. "Some conditions were worse than we anticipated, particularly in the security area," acknowledges Deputy Defense Secretary Paul Wolfowitz. Richard Armitage, the radical right's number two at State, now wants the U.N. to get involved. The Defense Policy Board's Richard Perle newly concedes that we should have prepared a postwar Iraqi government. "The answer is to hand over power to Iraqis as soon as possible," says Perle.

Getting warmer...but still wrong.

The real answer is to get the hell out before one more American or Iraqi gets killed in a lost cause. "Leaving now would place Iraqis under violent usurpers and set a precedent that could haunt the U.S. government for years," argues the *New York Times*' Christopher Marquis, but we've already blown our chance to make a good first impression. More money, more men, more international involvement—those were good ideas back in March. Now it's too late to avoid the ostracism of the United States or the Afghanistanization of Iraq.

For God's sake, cut our losses—and Iraq's—and bring our troops home.

Anatomy of a Lie

On the assumption that America is thoroughly brainwashed, President Bush said with no hint of shame, "We've had no evidence that Saddam Hussein was involved in September the 11th." National Security Adviser Condoleezza Rice said, "We have never claimed that Saddam Hussein had either...direction or control of 9/11." Defense Secretary Donald Rumsfeld said, "I've not seen any indication that would lead me to believe I could say" that Saddam Hussein was tied to the terrorist attacks of September 11, 2001.

These statements were meant to drown out Vice President Dick Cheney. With public support sagging for the Iraq quagmire, Cheney recently tried to restore legitimacy to the invasion and occupation by resurrecting the discounted claim that top 9/11 hijacker Mohammed Atta met with an Iraqi intelligence agent five months before the attacks. Cheney said the invasion "struck a major blow right at the heart of the base, if you will, the geographic base of the terrorists who have had us under assault now for many years, but most especially on 9/11."

Cheney was doing what Bush, Rice, and Rumsfeld did all along. To date, 304 American soldiers and thousands of Iraqi soldiers and civilians are dead because the White House riled up Americans into a rash blurring of the facts until they could no longer distinguish September 11 from Saddam.
—Derrick Z. Jackson, Boston Globe, September 24, 2003

OCTOBER 14, 2003—On September 18, 2003, George W. Bush finally realized that his lies had gone too far. A *Washington Post* poll showed that, thanks to his statements, 70 percent of Americans thought that Saddam Hussein—not Osama bin Laden—was behind 9/11. With the press leaning on him to put up some evidence or 'fess up to lying, he ordered his henchmen to backpedal. Asked whether there was a link between Saddam and 9/11, Donald Rumsfeld said: "I've not seen any indication that would lead me to believe that I could say that." Bush chimed in: "We've had no evidence that Saddam Hussein was involved with September the 11th. "We have never claimed that Saddam Hussein...had either direction or control of 9/11," affirmed Condoleeza Rice.

Along with his $87 billion request to Congress for Iraq spending, his admitting the

lack of a Saddam–Osama connection caused Bush's ABC News approval rating to plummet from 58 percent in September to 47 percent in October. The truth didn't play well. Therefore, relying on H.L. Mencken's observation that no one ever went broke overestimating the stupidity of the American public, Bush has returned to the same old lies he has already admitted.

On October 10, without offering a smidgen of new evidence, Dick Cheney again asserted a connection between 9/11 and Operation Iraqi Fiefdom. "Iraq has become the central front in the war on terror. Our mission in Iraq is a great undertaking and part of a larger mission that the United States accepted now more than two years ago. September 11, 2001 changed everything for this country."

Although no evidence of weapons of mass destruction has been found in Iraq, Cheney also reverted to the White House's pre-war argument for preemptive invasion: "We could not accept the grave danger of Saddam Hussein and his terrorist allies turning weapons of mass destruction against us or our friends or allies." Saddam = terrorism = 9/11 but worse.

According to the U.N. International Labor Organization, we Americans work longer hours than any other nation in the industrialized world. As White House TV guru Greg Jenkins says, "Americans are leading busy lives, and sometimes they don't have the opportunity to read a story or listen to an entire broadcast. But if they can have an instant understanding of what the president is talking about by seeing sixty seconds of television, you accomplish your goals as communicators." People don't have time for the facts, much less nuance.

The Bushies exploit our stress to blur the fictional link between Iraq and 9/11. Let's dissect Cheney's key argument: "We could not accept the grave danger of Saddam

Hussein and his terrorist allies turning weapons of mass destruction against us or our friends or allies."

The "danger," according to the Vice Resident, came from Saddam and his "terrorist allies." But Saddam didn't have WMDs. Bush's own chief weapons inspector says so. That leaves Saddam's "terrorist allies."

Here's where the disconnect gets interesting. When post-9/11 Americans think of "terrorists," they think of Osama bin Laden and al-Qaeda. But when Bush officials talk about Saddam's links to "terrorism," they're referring to something quite different: Hamas, Hezbollah and Islamic Jihad, the Palestinian groups fighting the Israeli occupation. Rumsfeld says: "We know he was giving $25,000 a family for anyone who would go out and kill innocent men, women and children." (By the way, this oft-repeated allegation has yet to be sourced or corroborated by a reputable journalist.) As usual, the spin is based on what they leave out: Rumsfeld wants to mislead you into thinking that those payments went to al-Qaeda to encourage them to blow up American men, women and children, perhaps on 9/11. In fact, the intended targets of Hamas, Hezbollah and Islamic Jihad are Israelis.

Hamas, Hezbollah and Islamic Jihad have carried out horrendous attacks in Israel. Many innocent people have been killed. But these groups don't have WMDs. And they've never indicated an interest in attacking Americans. Had Cheney told the truth, it would have gone something like this: "We could not accept the possibility of Saddam Hussein's Palestinian terrorist allies financing suicide bombers against Israel." Or, more succinctly: "We must take out Saddam because he indirectly finances attacks against our ally, Israel."

Many Americans support Israel, but very few would send U.S. troops to fight Ariel

Sharon's war against the Palestinians.

The Bushies' arguments inevitably fall apart upon close inspection. Now Condi Rice is backtracking from *her* backtrack: Saddam had to go, she says, because he posed a threat from "a region from which the 9/11 threat emerged." Guilt by geographical proximity, evidently, is enough to justify carpet-bombing. Israel also happens to be in the Middle East. Should we attack her too?

On September 18, Bush thought it would help to admit the truth: that Saddam Hussein had never been a threat to the United States. But less than a month later, when the press had moved on to other stories in its news cycle, he reverted to form. On October 9, Bush's polls upticked as he argued once again: "I was not about to leave the security of the American people to a madman."

It's too late for that.

THE YEAR OF THE LONG KNIVES

The Necropublican National Convention

President Bush's advisers have drafted a re-election strategy built around raising $200 million and staging the latest nominating convention in the Republican Party's history. The timing will allow Bush to begin his formal campaign near the third anniversary of September 11 and, supporters hope, enhance his fund-raising advantage.

The president is planning a sprint of a campaign that would start, at least officially, with his acceptance speech at the Republican convention, now set for September 2. The convention, to be held in New York City, will be the latest since the Republican Party was founded in 1856, and Bush's advisers said they chose the date so the event would flow into the commemorations marking the third anniversary of the World Trade Center attacks.

—Adam Nagourney and Richard W. Stevenson,
New York Times, April 22, 2003

OCTOBER 28, 2003—Next year, for the first time ever, Republicans will hold their national convention in New York City, the high temple of American liberalism. At a time when Americans are politically polarized over Iraq and other divisive issues, Republicans plan to nominate an extreme right-winger in a city where 81 percent of the locals voted for Al Gore. To top it off, they're scheduling their Roy-in-the-lion's-mouth act in September—the GOP usually holds its confabs in July—to coincide with ceremonies commemorating the 9/11 attacks.

At the risk of coming off like those who warned that President Clinton risked his life every time he appeared before audiences of well-armed soldiers on Southern military bases, let me say, as a New Yorker: this is a very bad idea.

"Next year in New York" is already the rallying cry of more than 150 groups planning to protest Bush's coronation. United for Peace and Justice, which organized some of the biggest demonstrations against the invasion of Iraq, has applied for a 250,000-person permit to march past Madison Square Garden, where the convention is being held, on the event's first full day.

Everyone from radical anarchists to moderate environmentalists expects the NYC/GOP

ideological collision to spark the biggest American protest march since the end of the Vietnam War. Families of 9/11 victims, predominantly Democratic like the oasis of ideological sanity they live in, are so incensed at reports that the convention was timed to allow Bush to lay the Freedom Tower cornerstone at the World Trade Center site that many plan to join the protest. "Keep your hands off Ground Zero," Rita Lasar, head of a 9/11 victims group, warns Republicans. "Do not make a political football out of this."

Too late. New York's Republican mayor and governor have denied the cornerstone-laying story, but they've confirmed that Bush will shuttle back and forth between the convention in midtown and speeches at Ground Zero. And Rudy Giuliani is encouraging convention organizers to use 9/11 as a prop.

Activists are talking, some with barely hidden glee, about the possibility of violence. "It'll be Chicago 1968," a well-connected progressive leader predicts, referring to the "Days of Rage" riots during that year's Democratic National Convention. "Things are gonna burn, people are gonna die." Harsh new NYPD tactics, like using horses to trample protesters, could throw gas on an already combustible situation. "Angry protesters have claimed police are meeting [antiwar] demonstrations with new heights of repressiveness, amounting to a pattern of unfounded arrests and abuses," reports the *Village Voice*.

Both sides are itching for a fight. "If they think New York City will welcome them with open arms, or even tolerate them dancing on the graves of the WTC victims, they are in for a very rude awakening," "Seraphiel" posted to the TalkLeft.com web site. "I hope it is a remake of the '68 convention in Chicago and the fabulous NYPD, this time, get to break some left-wing heads like grapes," a Bush supporter named "David" responded.

As much as I relish the idea of a million angry Americans turning the tawdry

Necropublican National Convention into a Seattle WTO-style fiasco, the potential for mayhem is terrifying. As a Manhattanite, I hope that the Republicans will seriously consider moving their convention somewhere else. New York, wounded by the dot-com crash and 9/11 (the latter injury exacerbated when Bush welched on the money he promised to help the city rebuild), continues to suffer from widespread unemployment. The risk of convention-related terrorist attacks should be reason enough to not hold it in a city that paid the highest price on 9/11. A revival of 1968, with cops fouling their batons with the blood of young people, wouldn't do anyone—left or right—any good.

Riots would make everyone look bad: New York, the GOP and the demonstrators. The resulting property damage could exceed the cost that would be involved in moving the convention to another city—a price that the well-funded Bush campaign can easily afford. The Bushies would be better off today if they had taken my advice on Afghanistan, Iraq and the economy. They've haven't listened yet—but that's no reason not to start now.

A Cold Draft

Defense officials are trying to dispel rumors that the military draft is returning. A routine notice on a Web site sparked rumors that the military may reinstitute conscription. "There are no secret discussions," a Selective Service spokesman said, adding that registration for the draft is "just an insurance policy" in case the country needs to mobilize. Officials say they just need to replace people who have left the nation's draft boards—and insist nothing unusual is afoot.

—Associated Press, November 11, 2003

DECEMBER 2, 2003—When I was a kid, standing around the post office waiting for my mom to buy stamps, I entertained myself by flipping through the "wanted" notices clipped to the bulletin board. I was impressed by the fact that most of the people who'd done bad things didn't look all that evil in their mug shots. Mostly the felons looked tired. And poor. You could tell from their frayed collars.

Mixed in with the accused murderers, kidnappers and mail fraud conspirators (this was the post office, after all) were local kids wanted for dodging the draft. Their profiles didn't look anything like those of men wanted for tri-state killing sprees. The sections dedicated to "prior convictions" were blank and the government didn't have fingerprints for them. Draft evaders' photos came from their high school yearbooks where everyone turned a little to the right, grinning with optimism and framed by shaggy early '70s haircuts. Nevertheless, the message was clear. As far as the government was concerned, evading service in Vietnam was as bad as boosting a bank.

Whenever the feds needed more cannon fodder, they interrupted primetime sit-coms to broadcast a draft lottery. Two guys wearing American flag lapel pins would turn a metal tumbler and pluck out slips of paper bearing birthdays from eighteen years earlier. "If you were born on April 4, 1951, you have thirty days to report to your local Selective Service bureau."

Shirley Jackson's short story "The Lottery" wasn't nearly as creepy.

"How long has this war been going on?" I asked my mom while Uncle Walt recited body counts along with the closing value of the Dow Jones Industrial Average. Born in 1963, I must have been about eight.

"Pretty much since you were born," she replied. Then she corrected herself. "Well, really even before that."

"Will it end before I turn eighteen?"

"I don't know. Probably not. I hope so."

They stopped the draft when I was ten; we lost the war two years later. I never had to resolve the terrible dilemma that drove those kids on the wanted posters to flee to Canada. Were they pacifists or were they wimps? Everyone knew that Vietnam wasn't winnable. Was it wrong to refuse to die for nothing, or was it good sense? Was defending the corrupt South Vietnamese regime of President Nguyen Van Thieu "fighting for your country"? Even if a war was both winnable and moral—World War II, say—was forcing a human being to risk death and dismemberment a form of slavery?

War is the riskiest and gravest endeavor that can be undertaken by a nation-state. Defensive combat, the struggle for self-preservation, is the only kind of war a just and prudent nation may wage. Unless an overwhelming majority of a country's citizens agrees that a war is necessary—a *real* war like Iraq or Vietnam, not a lark like Grenada or Panama—it cannot be won. And a country united by the consensus that it must fight doesn't need a draft. Citizens will line up to volunteer.

In early November, the Pentagon web site DefendAmerica.mil put out a call for applicants willing to serve on Selective Service System draft boards. "Serve Your Community and the Nation—Become a Selective Service System Local Board Member," the ad read. "If a military draft becomes necessary, approximately 2,000 local and appeal boards throughout America would decide which young men who submit a claim receive deferments, postponements or exemptions from military service, based on federal guidelines."

Noting that the SSS hopes to fill its 8,000 draft board slots by spring 2005, many journalists are wondering aloud whether the Bush Administration plans to reinstate forced con-

scription of 18-to-26-year-olds after the election, just in time for invasions of Iran, Syria and/or North Korea.

Reports of a big uptick in the draft agency's budget from '03 to '04 abound, yet the feds claim that ramping up Selective Service is part of "the routine cycle of things."

"There are no secret discussions," says SSS spokesman Pat Schuback. "We aren't doing any planning that we don't do on a routine basis." Yet they refuse to issue a categorical denial. A February Surprise, perhaps?

Our armed forces are stretched dangerously thin. 60,000 of the 130,000 troops stationed in Iraq come from the National Guard or reserves. 90,000 more are serving in Kuwait, Afghanistan, South Korea, Kosovo and Macedonia. Demoralized by low pay and long tours of duty under harsh conditions—why won't Bush invade someplace with nice weather and hot babes?—49 percent of soldiers told *Stars and Stripes* newspaper that they won't re-enlist. Defense Secretary Donald Rumsfeld and top brass say they prefer volunteer professionals to surly conscripts, but in the end they may not have a choice.

This much is certain: If Bush resumes his neocolonial landgrab after "re"election, he'll have to bring back the draft. And a new generation of young men, ordered to disrupt their lives to feed the vanity and bank accounts of a cabal of gangsters, will ponder whether to flee or fight.

Get Out of Iraq While the Getting's Good

Excerpts from a speech by the author to the Yale Political Union
in New Haven, Connecticut, on December 4, 2003

Thank you for inviting me here tonight. As someone who has been both expelled by and graduated with honors from Columbia University, a place you rarely think about, I know that you'll accept the sympathies that I'd like to offer on behalf of a beloved Yalie George W. Bush. My condolences are exactly as sincere as they are chock full of detached bemusement. Sadly, this middle-aged white man, once so full of promise and now filled to the brim with the waste product of a wasted life, finds himself, in the immortal closing voiceover from Kubrick's *Full Metal Jacket*, in a world of shit.

Of course, Governor Bush's situation is a desperate one. As he begins campaigning to win his first legal election, a race that pollsters predict will be nearly as tight as the last one, Bush's economy has bled more than three million jobs. But the news isn't all bad. He has also created three million freshly minted Democrats. As this year's budget deficit has skyrocketed, even his long-suffering Congressional lapdogs are considering cutting up his credit cards. Worst of all, of course, the war in Iraq—which was an uphill battle to begin with—has been irretrievably lost.

Whether the voters send Bush back to Crawford in January 2005 is of marginal importance to anyone but his major campaign contributors. Whether the United States of America strengthens or fades away, however, means everything.

No politician or political party is worth allowing harm to befall the greatest experiment in representative democracy ever undertaken. One man's fate pales next to the risk of threatening the security of the world's sole remaining superpower, its largest economy and the cornerstone of international stability. George W. Bush may save his presidency, or more accurately win what he stole, by following my advice to pull out of Iraq. But Bush doesn't matter. What matters to you and me is the national security of our wonderful country, and that interest would be best served by an immediate American troop withdrawal from occupied Iraq.

The costs of invading and occupying Iraq have been enormous. As of yesterday, 434 American and about 100 coalition soldiers have died in combat, accidents and "friendly fire" incidents; several thousand have been grievously wounded. CNN estimates that 3,500 Iraqi civilians died during the invasion; because the Pentagon refuses to keep a tally of Iraqi casu-

alties during the current guerrilla war, it's impossible to determine how many Iraqis have died since. There have been countless deaths of innocent Iraqis, including this past Sunday, when U.S. forces reported killing 54 Iraqi "insurgents" in Samarra. Most turned out to be civilians, including a local teacher and two Iranian pilgrims. According to the Associated Press, "Many residents said Saddam loyalists attacked the Americans, but that when U.S. forces began firing at random, many civilians got their guns and joined the fight. Many said residents were bitter about recent U.S. raids in the night."

No one talks about the Iraqi soldiers who died in battle, performing their duty against a better-armed force, but the Department of Defense guesstimates those losses at anywhere between 20,000 and 50,000 men. They were husbands, fathers, brothers and sons. If you travel into combat zones, as I did a few years ago to Afghanistan, you'll quickly forget the distinction between our victims and their victims. They were human beings, just like ours. Few if any were "terrorists."

The Pentagon, which Congress recently appropriated $1 billion for Afghanistan and $86 billion to occupy and rebuild Iraq, freely acknowledges that Congress has merely made a downpayment on the sandy killing fields. At a monthly cost of $1 to $2 billion, plus Halliburton's exorbitant estimates of the price of restoring oil and other infrastructure, the *lowest* estimate for a five-year occupation is currently running at a whopping $500 billion. If Bush ordered a pullout today, the United States could nationalize its colleges and universities and allow every student in the country, including here at Yale, to pay zero tuition—yet still come out ahead. And that's not accounting for interest. Bush's tax cuts and new Homeland Security bureaucracy helped turn President Clinton's estimated $4 trillion projected ten-year federal budget surplus into a $6 trillion deficit. We don't have the money for this war. We're borrowing it by issuing Treasury bonds and notes to foreign investors. Even if we keep the occupation under budget, which would make this the first-ever case of government avoiding budget overruns, we're going to lay out a hell of lot more than half a trillion dollars before this is all over.

Expense alone, however, should not preclude the United States from waging war. No one would say that it wasn't worth the enormous price we paid to destroy Nazi Germany, fascist Italy or imperial Japan. Of course, Bush tried to make the case. Taking on Iraq, he tried to convince us, would be like fighting World War II all over again. Saddam Hussein, he told us, was the Adolf Hitler of the Middle East. Some of my editorial cartoonist colleagues helped out by drawing the Iraqi dictator with a teeny Bavarian mustache, but the analogy still didn't play.

Saddam, Bush said, had invaded his neighbors and gassed his own people. What went unspoken was that he'd attacked Iran on behalf of Ronald Reagan, when he was still working as a U.S. puppet. Or that, as the U.S. has done so often and continues to do in places like Central Asia, we looked away as our valuable "strategic ally" brutalized Iraq's Kurdish minority. True, since invading Kuwait and being driven out by a U.S.-led coalition in 1991, Saddam Hussein had presided over a violent and despotic dictatorship. In that he was no different from such U.S. allies in our so-called "war on terror" as Saparmurat Niyazov, Islam Karimov, Nursultan Nazarbayev and General Pervez Musharraf. But Iraq hadn't invaded anyone since 1990, which is further back than most Americans can remember.

The failure of the Saddam-as-Hitler argument led to the Bush Administration's repeated claim that Saddam possessed weapons of mass destruction and planned to use them against the U.S. and its allies—perhaps Israel and Saudi Arabia. Here are just a few of the

lines Administration officials used in their build-up to war:

Dick Cheney, speaking to the VFW national convention on August 26, 2002: "Simply stated, there is no doubt that Saddam Hussein now has weapons of mass destruction."

George Bush, addressing the UN General Assembly on September 12: "Right now, Iraq is expanding and improving facilities that were used for the production of biological weapons."

Ari Fleischer, at a January 9 briefing: "We know for a fact that there are weapons there."

Bush's State of the Union Address on January 28: "Our intelligence officials estimate that Saddam Hussein had the materials to produce as much as five hundred tons of sarin, mustard and VX nerve agent."

Colin Powell, to the UN Security Council, on February 5: "We know that Saddam Hussein is determined to keep his weapons of mass destruction, is determined to make more."

Bush, in a March 17 speech to the nation: "Intelligence gathered by this and other governments leaves no doubt that the Iraq regime continues to possess and conceal some of the most lethal weapons ever devised."

I could go on—Lord, could I go on—but my voice and your patience wouldn't outlast a full reading of these statements.

Iraq's longest-range missiles could only travel a maximum range of 400 miles, by the way. I'm thinking that maybe Saddam planned to FedEx them to Washington. Anyway, Secretary of State Colin Powell delivered a laundry list of weapons, down to the exact number of liters of anthrax medium, that the United Nations would find in Iraq should it choose to validate America's crusade by committing troops. Defense Secretary Donald Rumsfeld told ABC on March 30 that he knew exactly where Saddam's WMDs were, naming sites and cities. "We know where they are," he said. "They're in the area around Tikrit and Baghdad and east, west, south and north somewhat." We know now that there weren't any WMDs in Iraq. We also know that the Bush Administration didn't even *think* it knew where they were. They made it all up, pulling bits and pieces from out-of-date CIA reports so they could blame "faulty intelligence" later on.

If Rumsfeld wasn't lying, why didn't U.S. weapons inspectors find nuclear, biological and/or chemical weapons where he said they'd be? When you state you know where something is and it doesn't turn up where you'd promised, you were lying. To be charitable, the best one can say for the White House's alleged "case" against Saddam Hussein is that, as of 1998—the most recent date for which reliable weapons information was available—Iraq had

chemical and perhaps biological weapons. On May 13, Major General David Petraeus, Commander of the 101st Airborne, became the first official to concede the truth: "I just don't know whether it was all destroyed years ago—I mean, there's no question that there were chemical weapons years ago—whether they were destroyed right before the war, [or] whether they're still hidden." As the *New York Times* has since reported, the WMDs probably were destroyed back in 1999, a fact that U.N. inspectors under Hans Blix would have verified had he been allowed to do so by a Bush Administration hell-bent on war. Ironically, Saddam believed that if he came clean about his compliance, he would appear defenseless.

In 1998 I owned a bootleg copy of the first Belle and Sebastian EP, but if recording industry cops broke down the door to my apartment, it wouldn't be there today. Knowing that Saddam had proscribed weapons in 1998 didn't mean that he had them in 2003. But, as Karl Rove and Dick Cheney are aware, it's tough to make the case for "imminent threat" based on archival data.

After testing various rationales for war, with the international community and many Americans continuing to balk, Bush rolled out his ultimate and ultimately baseless charge: Saddam Hussein, he and his cabinet members implied so often that 70 percent of the public accepted it as Gospel truth, had planned and carried out 9/11. Not Osama. Not the Saudis. Saddam. The Bushies backed off from this gigantic, jumbo-sized lie under pressure from the media, but as soon as the journos stopped paying attention (which seems to happen a lot nowadays) they were back at it.

But you already knew all that. Bush's litany of lies is old news to those of us who make an effort to stay informed. The rest of the world hasn't moved on, though. For our traditional allies like France and Germany, as well as individuals both Muslim and otherwise, Bush's brazen falsehoods to justify war will forever color the subsequent occupation. Even if the Iraqi people had greeted us with wine and roses, even if all the news from Baghdad were positive, they would never accept Bush's ends-justify-the-means approach to preemptive warfare—or more accurately, arbitrary warfare.

War is a nation-state's most extreme undertaking. It must be entered into seriously, not with smirks and fake cowpoke rhetoric. For war to be considered legitimate, it must be presented as a desperate last resort for self-preservation rather than the continuation of diplomacy—or the expansion of commerce—by other means. An overwhelming majority of people must be convinced that there is no other choice. The arguments used to build consensus for conflict must be truthful in form as well as substance. Otherwise you end up with Vietnam, which "began" with a fictional attack on a U.S. destroyer in the Tonkin Gulf.

Speaking on the *U.S.S. Abraham Lincoln* on May 2, Bush said that "The use of force has been and remains our last resort." Yet another lie. There was no justification and no national consensus for Gulf War II—and it certainly wasn't a last resort. And that may be reason enough to pull out now. No matter how you see the war, as a well-intentioned mistake based on flawed intelligence or as a cynical, evil gambit to carry out a plan called the Project for a New American Century, hatched by Dick Cheney, Condoleezza Rice and Richard Perle before Bush came to power, the U.S. never enjoyed a tacit, legitimately constructed consensus at home or abroad that what it was doing was necessary or justified. Lies, Governor Bush, do matter.

Now that we've got more than 130,000 soldiers occupying Iraq, don't we have an obligation to finish the job? If we pull out now, won't Iraq disintegrate? How can we tell the widows and widowers of American soldiers that their loved ones died for nothing?

No. Yes. And we have no choice.

Since there weren't any WMDs, we obviously don't need to stay in Iraq to destroy nonexistent weapons. That leaves the *fait accompli* argument, which falls flat on its face. The only reason for the U.S. to remain in Iraq, as provided by either Administration apologists or pro-war liberals like Thomas Friedman, is to plant the seed of democracy in the Middle East. Under this model, victory in Iraq—from the U.S. perspective—requires establishing sufficient peace and tranquility in the streets and alleys of Iraq to create conditions where democracy and free enterprise can flourish. A post-Baath Party democracy would bring Sunnis, Shiites, Turcomen and Kurds under the umbrella of a vibrant multiparty Iraqi federation. Presumably, the long-oppressed citizens of neighboring Arab states, watching the happy news on Al Jazeera, would agitate for change, which would force some regimes to reform and spark velvet revolutions against others. One wonders what the Kuwaitis think of this idea, but that's the vision of the neo-conservatives.

Trouble is, it's impossible.

First of all, there is no such thing as Iraq anymore. The Kurds have enjoyed *de facto* autonomy since the early 1990s. They have their own currency, stamps and national anthem, and they've made it clear that they're never coming back. Earlier this year U.S. invasion forces, by failing to force Kurdistan back into Iraq, ratified the nation's permanent partition into at least two states: a future Republic of Kurdistan and a rump Iraq. Furthermore, our policy of deBaathification is alienating the forty percent Sunni minority by depriving anyone who joined the party under the deposed regime of the right to earn a living. Desperation is growing. Civil war, Iraqis on both sides of the Sunni-Shia divide agree, is probably inevitable.

Neighboring states, in particular Turkey and Iran, are also playing a destabilizing role within Iraq. Turkey, fearful of renewed pro-independence agitation from its own Kurdish minority, is funding Sunni factions operating in Mosul and other border areas along the northern "green line" between Kurdistan and Iraq proper. Iranian hardliners, meanwhile, believe that they see the future of Iraq—and that it looks a lot like Teheran circa 1978. In Iraqi politics, tribe and clan affiliation have always been a preeminent determinant. Even in an ideal Jeffersonian-style democracy, Iraq's sixty percent Shiite majority will enjoy continuous dominance, creating a perpetually neglected and/or abused Sunni minority. The American-led deBaathification policy pushes demography to further extremes of social polarization. The U.S. has made little or no effort to contain street violence, tacitly condoning revenge killings of leading Sunnis. As Iraqi clerics return from exile in Iran and their fun-

THE SHAREHOLDERS OF THE BECHTEL GROUP, INC., FLUOR CORP., LOUIS BERGER GROUP INC., PARSONS CORP., BOOTS & COOTS INTERNATIONAL WELL CONTROL INC. AND KELLOGG, BROWN & ROOT, A SUBSIDIARY OF HALLIBURTON CO., DICK CHENEY, PROPRIETOR

THANK THE MEN AND WOMEN OF THE U.S. ARMED FORCES.

We salute those who made the ultimate sacrifice.

©2003 TEDRALL

damentalist allies provide funding for agitation, Iraq's secular status is being eroded daily. The not-so-great irony is that a liberalizing Iran, whose overtures have been repeatedly rebuffed by the Bush Administration, is financing a radical Shiite revolution in Iraq.

The antiwar left accuses the Bush Administration of failing to prepare a plan for post-war Iraq, but that's not strictly true. The Pentagon's plan, as it has been in previous wars, was to stand by and let things develop, to see which factions—among the State and Defense Department-approved lists of anti-Baath Iraqi exile groups—would ultimately emerge with popular support. Top officials were warned that, *après Saddam, le deluge*, but they couldn't believe it. The removal of a strongman with more than two decades to consolidate power created a power vacuum which no one, least of all Ahmed Chalabi (who left Iraq at the age of twelve), could fill.

We can't put the toothpaste back into the tube.

We might have avoided some of the current problems by preparing a successor government and taking steps to prevent looting and random violence. Inexplicably the Defense Department refused to allow U.S. Army civil affairs detachments to cross the border from Kuwait until after the worst rioting was already underway. You only get one chance to make a good first impression, and we blew it.

Then, after we failed to install or find a viable pro-American post-Saddam regime, various insurgent groups—former regime figures, Shiite radicals, Islamist guerrillas and even Kurds—perceived a chance to seize control for themselves. Unfortunately, they can't fight each other until they get rid of us. Like the diverse component groups allied to form the French Resistance during World War II, they're united in a marriage of convenience, one that's launching an average of 35 attacks daily and dedicated to killing so many Americans that the U.S. public withdraws its support for the occupation. Our policy of overwhelming retaliation, ranging from arbitrary arrests of Iraqis said to be anti-American, to humiliating searches of homes and pat-downs of wives and daughters, to bombing cities located near ambush sites, is killing and maiming countless innocents. It's playing into the hands of the resistance. It didn't work for the French in Algeria. Ask any Israeli whether the politics of retaliation are effective in the Occupied Territories. The more clumsily and aggressively we react to attacks by Iraqi resistance fighters, the more angry recruits they find among an increasingly radicalized population. The most effective way to build popular support, by killing Iraqis with kindness, seems neither likely nor feasible. Ours is a poorly-trained occupation army largely composed of uneducated young men who never traveled before they enlisted. They neither speak Arabic nor understand the complex tribal and religious politics

of the country they're attempting to run. If you've been to the Middle East, you can't help but shudder with shame and disgust at the sight of men awaiting interrogation with gunny sacks over their heads as laughing soldiers pat down their wives and daughters. It isn't right; even worse, it's downright dumb. With U.S. troops coming under daily attack, however, sympathy and understanding are in short supply.

The resistance knows that it's winning. It possesses a huge stockpile of weapons and significant funding, with more of both pouring in across poorly guarded borders with Syria and Iran. Resistance forces are operating on their home turf. Time is on their side, but not on ours. During the 20th century, no nation has ever invaded another sovereign state and kept it for long. Iraq is not likely to become the first exception. The last time we fought a war on as large a scale as Iraq, indigenous fighters drove us out of Vietnam. Make no mistake: the Iraqi resistance thinks they're going to win the same way, applying the same ruthless dedication and relentlessness some of them used against the Soviets in Afghanistan, and they're probably right. Retired General Theodore Mataxis wrote the following in the forward to the Russian army's review of its Afghan war: "What guerrillas do not need is military victory. Guerrillas need to survive and endure over the years or decades of the conflict". The winning side in such a war prevails, he wrote, "because of higher morale, greater obstinacy, stronger national will, and the determination to survive."

Wanna bet which side has all of the above in Iraq?

When evaluating the feasibility of continuing to fight in Iraq, we shouldn't ignore the danger of contributing to the spread of regional and international instability. As I've mentioned, Turkey is nervously eying its southeast as the possible site of another bloody civil conflict or border war with a nascent Kurdish state. On the brink of bankruptcy and threatened by rising Islamic fundamentalism, Turkey is the strategic linchpin between Europe and Asia, a crucial ally to Israel and the U.S., and the highest civilized achievement of secular Islam. The former Soviet republics of Central Asia are currently wavering between following Ankarra and Islamabad as their model, and the world's largest untapped oil reserves—six times more than Saudi Arabia—hang in the balance. If Turkey disintegrates as a result of the Kurdish/Iraqi conflict, revolution could spread like a wildfire across the Caucasus, the Balkans and even Eastern Europe.

Furthermore, Bush's preemptive war doctrine is encouraging nuclear proliferation. Nations that merely flirted with acquiring nukes until they "let" themselves be bought off not to go all the way have drawn the obvious conclusion from the invasion of Iraq: once Bush

THE LAW OF CONSERVATION OF DEMOCRACY

gets his teeth in your ass, nothing you can say or do will make him let go. Kim Jong Il of North Korea ramped up his nuke program in the days leading up to the invasion of Iraq, and may have built as many as four completed warheads. He has threatened a nuclear attack on the West Coast of the United States, and Bush has all but promised a non-aggression treaty as a reward—er, result. Iran may follow suit. We want the world to see al-Qaeda as the biggest threat to world peace, but the world sees *us* starting all the wars. Nukes look like the perfect antidote to American militarism.

Finally, we don't have enough troops to remain in Iraq. As things stand, the U.S. only employs about a quarter million men and women in combat positions in its standing volunteer army. 130,000 are in Iraq, with 20,000 more on the way. 10,000 are in Kabul. We've got 30,000 more scattered around the world, not including those stationed in the Korean demilitarized zone. National Guard and reserve units are stretched beyond their limits. If we were attacked by a real foe, by an enemy that truly possessed weapons of mass destruction, we wouldn't be able to defend ourselves. Rumor has it that the Selective Service System is gearing up for a new draft to begin after the election in 2005. But, as the army learned during Vietnam, resentful draftees are no substitute for professional volunteer soldiers with years of training and experience.

The war in Iraq is sapping wealth and manpower, as well as political focus, from a real war on terrorism, a war that we never began in earnest. Two years and three months ago, nineteen Saudi and Egyptian hijackers murdered more than three thousand Americans in New York, Washington and Pennsylvania. To this day, the Administration has made next to no effort whatsoever to bring the organizations that planned and carried out those attacks to justice. The nations that funded and harbored the criminals, countries which would have made more appropriate targets of American military action than Afghanistan or Iraq—despotic regimes in Saudi Arabia, Pakistan and Egypt—have enjoyed increased American aid since 9/11. The criminals remain free while we bog down our troops with a war that is so pointless that even its real objective—securing strategic dominance over the second largest oil reserves on earth—remains elusive.

Someday the U.S. will realize that the cost of occupying Iraq to fight its people far outweighs the potential benefits of a democratized Middle East. We will inevitably conclude, moreover, that our stated war aims—peace and stability, unity and democracy—are unachievable given the situation in Iraq and the nature of our strategy. Gulf War II was lost the day it was conceived; the only question is how long it will take for an American president to accept the truth and order a withdrawal.

Yes, Iraq will probably fall apart. A Shiite revolution is likely. Iraqis and other Arabs will despise us for replacing Saddam Hussein with something even worse: lawlessness and chaos. It's awful and it is our fault, but nothing can be done about this mess now. No one can save the occupation, but there would be some long-term benefits of leaving Iraq. Were we to admit to the United Nations and the world that we committed a grave error of miscalculation and hubris when we began dropping bombs on Baghdad, it might begin to humanize us. Until now, being American has always meant never having to say we're sorry.

Thousands of people, some innocent and some not, have died for this fraud of a war. It's already obvious to all but the most pigheaded that, sooner or later, we will abandon Iraq just as we've abandoned Afghanistan. Why prolong the pain? Let's cut our losses and get out now. Everyone who has lost their lives in Iraq has died for Bush's lies. Everyone who dies from this day forward will die for nothing.

Weasels of Crass Deception

The economy and health care will dominate President Bush's domestic agenda for 2003, aides and experts say, but what gets accomplished in those areas could well hinge on challenges overseas, including the Iraq issue and the war on terrorism. "The economy is a huge issue," said White House adviser Mary Matalin, who left her post at the close of the year. "Peace and prosperity. That is why the president will offer — even before the Congress comes back likely — a growth package for investors and consumers and the market." The president is to lay out his agenda in detail in his State of the Union address in January.

—CNN, January 1, 2003

DECEMBER 23, 2003—Somebody at Homeland Security must have slipped the manuscript of my next book to Karl Rove. Among other things, my upcoming political manifesto posits that the Republicans won't be able to surf the 9/11-generated shock-and-awe wave forever. It's still the economy, stupid; it always will be. All the foreign policy successes in the world—catching Saddam, terrorizing Libya into unilateral disarmament, dragging Osama's bloated carcass down K Street—won't make three million people forget that they've lost their jobs or that Bush, whose estimated net worth runs between $9,634,088 and $26,593,000, refused to extend their unemployment checks.

Unless there's another dramatic attack in 2004, domestic issues will determine what happens in November.

Word has it that Bush will kick off his "re"election campaign with a package of domestic economic proposals to be announced during next month's State of the Union address. What the GOP calls "The Ownership Society," writes conservative *New York Times* pundit David Brooks, will "embrace the more productive and fluid economy, but make sure government aggressively moves to give workers the tools they need to cope."

"The Ownership Society," which acknowledges that most people change employers and careers throughout their working lives, shows that conservatives have been doing some creative thinking about their domestic agenda. Among the highlights:

Portable Health Insurance: Tax credits would subsidize medical premiums, the number of people who qualify for existing government programs like Medicare would be expanded, and small businesses would be allowed to form pools so their employees would qualify for group plans.

Reemployment Accounts: Unemployment stipends would be replaced by lump-sum personal "accounts" that layoff victims could spend, says Brooks, "on training, child care, a car, a move to a place with more jobs, or whatever else they think would benefit them."

Privatizing Social Security: This idea has been around for years. You would decide where to invest the money in your Social Security "account," like employees do now with their 401(k)s. As with a 401(k), you would reap big rewards during stock market booms but risk getting wiped out in a crash.

Except for Social Security privatization, which would excessively endanger retirement funds to line the pockets of politically connected Wall Street brokerage houses, these are interesting ideas—in theory. If you take a closer look, however, reality asks a lot of tough questions.

Bush says he wants Americans to adopt a "responsibility culture." But his Ownership Society concept requires more responsibility than most folks should be asked to bear. The health insurance tax credit, for example, would come in the form of a big refund check after taxpayers file their 1040s. Many workers, hit hard by stagnating wages and unexpected expenses, will spend the government windfall on other bills. The same thing goes for reemployment accounts. If a guy blows his lump-sum unemployment payment on a casino riverboat or Internet gaming-site bender, he and his family could end up out on the street. You and me, we might spend the money on computer classes. But for too many people, it's too big a temptation.

Worse still, the GOP's track record suggests that Bush's Ownership Society would merely replace the antiquated liberal safety net—which assumes that a person works for the same employer his or her entire life—with a privatized system that's so poorly underfinanced

as to be worthless. The much-ballyhooed No Child Left Behind Act has been, well, left behind—it hasn't received a penny. Bush welshed on his promise to spend $15 billion on African AIDS prevention. The average dollar value of the school vouchers issued by Cleveland, whose program Republicans say should be copied nationally, is so low that parents can't afford to move their kids to private schools. And the average taxpayer will receive just $800 from Bush's tax cuts—enough to bankrupt the treasury but not to stimulate the economy.

"Congress and the administration are looking at proposals that cost $50 billion to $80 billion over 10 years," the *Times* says. But that's chump change next to the size of the problems they claim to address. $8 billion per year would provide healthcare to just *three percent* of America's 44 million uninsured. And it wouldn't leave anything for reemployment accounts.

The only way to fund this election-year vote grab would be to cancel the $1.8 trillion tax cuts and the $100 billion-per-year occupation of Iraq—but Republicans aren't *that* serious.

"The public is not expecting perfection, but is looking for progress," says GOP pollster David Winston. Perhaps he's right—maybe the American people will view three percent as "progress." But where I come from, three percent ain't even a tip.

Pipe Dreams: An Update on the Real Reason We Invaded Afghanistan

Pakistan, Afghanistan and Turkmenistan signed a $2 billion deal Thursday to bring natural gas from Central to South Asia. Starting from the Daulatabad gas field in Turkmenistan, the nearly 1,000-mile pipeline is to pass through Afghanistan before entering Pakistan.

—*United Press International, May 31, 2002*

JANUARY 6, 2004—So where's the pipeline?

In 2001 common sense, expert opinion and extensive research convinced me and other Central Asia watchers that the United States didn't have much interest in saving Buddha statues or Afghan women when it went to war against the Taliban. After we turned down their offer to extradite Osama, it became obvious that we weren't interested in capturing the alleged mastermind of 9/11 either. Logic and evidence indicated that the Bush Administration focused on Afghanistan to make it secure for a pipeline to carry oil and natural gas from the landlocked Caspian Sea.

Here's the story in a nutshell. The former Soviet republics surrounding the Caspian Sea—particularly Kazakhstan—have the potential to become the biggest oil-producing nations on earth. "By 2050," reports the *Asia Times*, "the Persian Gulf/Caspian Sea will account for more than 80 percent of world oil and natural gas production. Together, the Persian Gulf and the Caspian may have something like 800 billion barrels of oil and an energy equivalent amount in natural gas. Compare this figure with oil reserves in the Americas and in Europe: less than 160 billion barrels. And they will be exhausted before 2030." Kazakhstan, Turkmenistan and Uzbekistan want to build a pipeline to carry their oil and gas out to deep-sea ports. The shortest possible route would go through Iran, which the U.S. has declared part of an Axis of Evil. Second shortest is via Afghanistan, a dangerous proposition that the Clinton and Bush Administrations have nonetheless encouraged during and after Taliban rule. Top Bushies last met with Taliban officials in July 2001, two months before 9/11. Negotiations broke down over transit fees, but top-level discussions between the U.S., Turkmenistan and Pakistan resumed in October, while American bombs were still raining on Kabul. That led people like me to speculate that the invasion—which made little effort to catch Osama—was a transparent excuse to gain control over newly emerging energy resources.

Yet here we are two years later, some war supporters point out, and still no pipeline. Well, not exactly.

It's not the sort of thing the U.S. media cares to report, but there has in fact been movement on the proposed Trans-Afghanistan Pipeline (TAP). The Asian Development Bank, which hopes to finance a consortium of oil companies to finance the $3.5 billion (originally $2 billion) project, has already spent millions of dollars on feasibility studies and surveys along the proposed route from Herat, a city near Afghanistan's northwest border with Turkmenistan, to Kandahar, the former Taliban spiritual capital close to the southeastern frontier with Pakistan. The U.S.-led occupation coalition has promised to make paving the future TAP service highway the nation's top rebuilding priority. The ADB has hosted meetings between officials of Afghanistan and the two nations on each end of the thousand-mile-long conduit: Turkmenistan, which would ship Kazakh crude oil and its own natural gas from its Daultebad refineries, and Pakistan, which hopes to export the energy resources to deep-sea tankers via its Multan port on the Arabian Sea.

Turkmen prime minister Yolly Gurganmuradov, Afghan minister of mines and industry Mehfooz Nedai and Pakistani petroleum minister Nouraiz Shakoor held their seventh TAP meeting in Islamabad on December 10 where they decided on a 2010 target date for completion. Official groundbreaking for TAP, predicted to occur last year during a rash of post-Mullah Omar optimism, now awaits verification that Pakistan can handle the anticipated volume of Turkmen gas. That study won't be completed until at least September 2004.

Far more worrisome is the Afghan government's dubious assurance that it "will provide complete security to the project," according to Pakistan's official news agency. The TAP route cuts through territory controlled by Herati warlord Ishmael Khan and several ex-Taliban commanders who would almost certainly threaten to blow it up unless they receive ad hoc "transit fees."

The challenges are virtually insurmountable, yet the three nations see reasons to justify working to meet a March 2004 financing deadline. A recent diplomatic thaw with India has opened up the possibility of extending the pipeline across Pakistan. "If Pakistan can find within itself the strength and wisdom to change its current approach towards India, there are immense benefits that it can derive as a transit route for the movement of energy, goods and people," Indian Foreign Minister Yashwant Sinha said January 3.

Even better, the star of TAP's biggest promoter—the U.S. Ambassador to Afghanistan —is rising. "Bush's pet Afghan" Zalmay Khalilzad, Karzai's ex-colleague at Unocal, is receiving kudos from grateful top Bushies. Last week the ubiquitous Khalilzad strong-armed delegates to the *loya jirga* into accepting a new constitution that ratifies Karzai's role as a U.S.-backed puppet dictator. TAP proponents hope Khalilzad's increased influence will convince Unocal and other U.S. companies to join the consortium.

I wrote about TAP as a motivation for the Afghan invasion in my book *Gas War*. The Bushies invaded Afghanistan to build a pipeline that would never be feasible, I argued. "Afghanistan remains a disaster zone," writes the Kyrgyz-based *Times of Central Asia* after the latest Islamabad confab. "All transnational projects somehow involving this war-weary country seem to be doomed with troubles. [TAP] is no exception."

Delays and overruns are typical for big construction projects, but based on the news so far there's no reason to change my 2001 assessment. Until we inevitably withdraw our forces a few years from now, once again abandoning the Afghans to a cycle of death and horror we helped perpetuate, Bush and his Asian allies will keep trying to build their doomed pipeline.

Finally, The Truth

A 400-strong US military team that has been searching for illicit weapons in Iraq has been withdrawn after finding nothing of substance, although a separate group looking for weapons of mass destruction still remains in the country, The New York Times reported on Thursday. "They picked up everything that was worth picking up," one US official told the daily, referring to the Joint Captured Materiel Exploitation Group, made up of technical experts headed by an unidentified Australian brigadier. The withdrawal of the 400-member military team was seen by some military officials as a sign that the US government may no longer expect to uncover chemical or biological weapons in Iraq, the daily said.
—Pakistan DAWN, January 9, 2004

JANUARY 13, 2004—Once again Bush and his top officials are responsible for an outrageous scandal whose monumental scale and grotesquely terrifying implications for our democracy make Watergate look like a fraternity prank. Yet the miscreants are getting away scot-free.

As usual.

The Bush Administration, reported the *New York Times* on January 8, "has quietly withdrawn from Iraq a 400-member military team whose job was to scour the country for military equipment. The step was described by some military officials as a sign that the administration might have lowered its sights and no longer expected to uncover the caches of chemical and biological weapons that the White House cited as a principal reason for going to war last March."

The Bushies have good reason to think they won't find any weapons of mass destruction in Iraq. They knew full well that the flimsy reports they used to sell their sleazy oil war were more than four years out of date—ancient history by intelligence standards. And, as the *Washington Post* writes, a newly discovered memo to Saddam Hussein indicates that Mr. Worse Than Hitler got rid of his WMDs in 1991. Unlike the United States, which unilaterally partitioned Iraq into no-fly zones and created a new Kurdish state, Saddam appears to have complied with the ceasefire agreement that ended the Gulf War.

The 1,400 members of the Iraq Survey Group have been searching for WMDs during the last seven months. They've spent hundreds of millions of dollars. They've been to every government installation in the country. They've come up empty-handed.

All we've gotten are numerous false alarms, each trumpeted as vindication of the Bushies' claim that Saddam would have nuked or gassed or poisoned us if we hadn't taken him out first. On May 31, Bush said: "You remember when Colin Powell stood up in front of the world, and he said Iraq has got laboratories, mobile labs to build biological weapons...we've so far discovered two. And we'll find more weapons as time goes on. But for those who say we haven't found the banned manufacturing devices or banned weapons, they're wrong. We found them."

Actually, we didn't find anything. Both "mobile labs" turned out to be rusted trailers used for filling weather balloons. But Bush's lies got so much more media coverage than subsequent attempts to set the record straight that all but the most press-obsessed were misled. By June 18, thirty-five percent of Americans told a Harris poll that they believed that we had already found WMDs in Iraq. And forty-eight percent thought that Bush's fictional link between Iraq and al-Qaeda had been "proven."

Iraq's WMDs were probably destroyed at least thirteen years ago. Fortunately for Bush, they exist only in the one place he cares about: the deluded minds of a terrifyingly ignorant American electorate.

Which is why our troops in Iraq are no longer bothering to go through the motions of searching for them. And why Bush yanked the Joint Captured Matériel Exploitation Group that was supposed to destroy WMDs if and when they had been discovered. "Its work was essentially done," a Defense Department official told the *Times*, because it was tired of "waiting for something to dispose of."

Nearly 500 American servicemen have been killed in the war against Iraq. At least 2,400 more have been wounded. We've killed so many Iraqis—tens of thousands, certainly—that

the Pentagon can't keep count. We've borrowed more than $160 billion to pay for this extravaganza, with many more hundreds of billions to follow. And what was the point of this waste of life and treasure? "To disarm Iraq," Bush told us.

But Iraq, as everyone from the CIA to Hans Blix to Saddam told us beforehand, didn't have any arms to dis. Calling off the WMD hunt is Bush's tacit admission that he lied about the reasons for war. It's hard to think of anything worse that a president can do. It's even harder to imagine the American people, so cynically accepting of deception, holding him accountable.

Suffer the French Schoolchildren

Surveys in recent months have shown enormous erosion of positive attitudes toward America. In Britain, a "favorable view of the U.S." declined to 70 percent from 83 percent, in Brazil to 34 percent from 56 percent, in France to 43 percent from 62 percent, in Morocco to 27 percent from 77 percent and in Turkey to 15 percent from 52 percent.
—Ted Pincus, Chicago Sun-Times, January 27, 2004

JANUARY 20, 2004—Why do they hate us? And where do they get their hatred from?

These questions haunted me and three other American visitors in Carquefou, France, as we studied a huge display of cartoons drawn by local schoolchildren assigned to convey their impressions of the United States. Panel after grisly panel depicted the United States, George Bush and those ubiquitous symbols of American commercial culture—McDonald's and Coke—as murderous, predatory and gleefully vicious. Obese Uncle Sams chopping up Iraqi children with a knife, their blood gushing across construction paper. A leering Statue of Liberty holding a hamburger in one hand while firing missiles at dying Afghan civilians across the ocean. The American flag, its bars transformed into prisons for the child inmates of Guantánamo. A baseball bat painted red, white and blue poised to smash a ball—which is a globe. The juxtaposition between the artwork's ferociously angry imagery and the childish drawing styles of the third graders would disturb the most jaded reader.

I didn't see a single positive portrayal of the U.S.

Organizers of Carquefou's annual cartoon art festival had invited four American artists—Steve Benson of the *Arizona Republic*, David Horsey of the *Seattle Post-Intelligencer*, Kal of the *Baltimore Sun* and yours truly—to this industrial town in conservative western France to discuss the deteriorated state of Franco-American relations. We've all used our cartoons to convey our dim opinion of the Bush Administration's domestic and foreign policy agenda. We oppose the war in Iraq. We despise the French bashing ("freedom fries," wine boycotts, high schools that have stopped teaching French) that has arisen since the Chirac government threatened to veto Bush's Iraq war resolution in the U.N. I even have dual French-American citizenship. We're a pretty liberal group; that's probably why they chose us.

We don't take issue with most of the cartoons' messages. They see Bush as a vicious, thoughtless warmonger with fascist tendencies, Americans as arrogant brutes who don't give a passing thought to the innocent people who die at the hands of their government and rapacious corporations as hegemonic steamrollers that crush cultural distinctiveness and independence in their ceaseless quest for the almighty dollar. They can't believe that we feel more entitled to use military force than Luxembourg or Monaco.

What must Palestinian kids think of us?

It would be nice to see these opinions expressed with more subtlety and nuance. But their opinions are more right than wrong. Americans believe they're exceptional. A Republican is someone who believes that we were right to invade Iraq. A Democrat is one who thinks we should have gone into Rwanda.

Still, walking past those drawings these past few days felt like getting slugged in the stomach. Part of it was the sheer scale—there were more than seven hundred pieces on display. But the level of rage and vitriol against America and everything related to it (one kid even trashed Tropicana orange juice) surpassed prewar propaganda in Saddam's Iraqi press. And these are kids. What a difference a hundred years makes: the Statue of Liberty, France's second great gift to America after freeing it from England, was funded by millions of *centimes* collected by French schoolchildren.

It pains you to see what Bush has done to our international reputation.

We repeatedly explained that there's more to the United States than George Bush. We pointed out that most voters supported Gore in the last election, that hundreds of thousands of Americans marched against the war. We argued that Americans are kind, big-hearted people. French attendees listened politely, and we were treated with the utmost kindness and hospitality, but their kids' cartoons screamed: we hate you.

That hurt.

Children get their politics from their parents and teachers, who form their impressions from the media. The European media has covered a different war than the one you've seen on CNN and Fox News. A 14-year-old Iraqi boy, shot by U.S. troops in Baghdad, was interviewed for five minutes on the evening news. "They did it on purpose," he said. "They were laughing." The bloody corpses of Iraqi civilians are standard TV fare here. The Bush Administration is routinely portrayed as greedy, stupid and mean.

Americans can find the truth about our nasty, unwinnable oil war, but they have to dig a little deeper. "The United States is using excessive power," Ghazi Ajil al-Yawar, a moderate, pro-American member of the Iraqi Governing Council, told the *New York Times Magazine* on January 11. "They round up people in a very humiliating way, by putting bags over their faces in front of their families. In our society, this is like rape. The Americans are using collective punishment by jailing relatives. What is the difference from Saddam? They are demolishing houses [of insurgents' family members] now. They say they want to teach a lesson to the people. But when Timothy McVeigh was convicted in the bombing in Oklahoma City, was his family's home destroyed?"

It's striking that al-Yawar knows McVeigh's name. How many Americans can identify any Iraqi other than Saddam Hussein? Most foreigners know more about us than we know about them. Hell, they know more about what we're doing in Iraq than we do ourselves.

Of course, many of us don't give a damn whether French schoolchildren or anyone else think Bush's United States is a land of butchers and thugs. Whether or not we care, however, it matters.

Don't Stop Bereaving

For all who love freedom and peace, the world without Saddam Hussein's regime is a better and safer place.
                                                    —George W. Bush, January 20, 2004

JANUARY 27, 2004—During his State of the Union address, George W. Bush exalted the liberation of the peoples of Afghanistan and Iraq from the tyranny of brutal and corrupt regimes. Bush recognizes that a lot of work remains to be done. "As long as the Middle East remains a place of tyranny, despair and anger," Bush said, "it will continue to produce men and movements that threaten the safety of America and our friends."

He's right. If we really want to win the war on terrorism, we've got to stop sitting around the Sunni triangle picking rose petals off our Kevlar jackets. If we're serious about liberation as a tool of terror prevention, we've got to invade every dictatorship, topple every autocracy and occupy every patch of soil where evil tyrants oppress their people, especially in the Muslim world.

Job one: Saudi Arabia. The country's evil monarchy financed 9/11, bans opposition parties and forces women to wear the *abaya* (identical to the Taliban's *burqa*) and doesn't even allow them to drive. According to Human Rights Watch, the Saudi Interior Ministry's General Directorate of Investigation subjects its political prisoners to "sexual harassment by threat or the actual practice [of] inserting an iron rod in the rectum." Bush says any dictator who runs "rape rooms" deserves execution. After we invade and replace his government with a democracy, therefore, George W. Bush should personally behead King Fahd (or stone him to death—these are the ways in which the Taliban-style Saudis execute their victims). Saudi Arabia is big but sparsely populated. Surely we have a spare 100,000 troops for the liberation of 23,000,000 Saudis.

Next, as Patton would say, on to the Arabian Sea! The long-suffering citizens of Yemen crave liberation from dictator Ali Abdallah Salih, whose vile Central Security and Political Security Office stormtroopers murder civilians at random. When an opposition candidate for local office dared to speak up recently, Salih's CS-PSO goons beat him to a pulp, shaved his head and bulldozed his house. Well, those days are over! We'll drive Salih into his local spider hole in no time. Then victorious U.S. troops can score some well-earned beachfront R-and-R.

While we're out democratizing, let's not forget those nasty little Gulf states: Bahrain, Kuwait, Oman, Qatar and the United Arab Emirates are run by a bunch of slave-trafficking, election-banning, opponent-torturing, democracy-despising kings, emirs and sultans.

We can take these despots out, easy—another 100,000 soldiers ought to do the job.

Of course, many republics of the former Soviet Union—places like Azerbaijan, Turkmenistan, Uzbekistan, Kyrgyzstan, Kazakhstan and Tajikistan—are Saddam-style dictatorships still run by the same Communist Party thugs who oppressed people under a different flag pre-1991. They use the former KGB to spy on dissidents, who are found dead, clearly bearing the marks of torture, or are simply "disappeared" entirely. The citizens of these regimes would welcome liberation.

In October, says Human Rights Watch, Azerbaijan's president Ilham Aliyev "carried out a well-organized campaign of [election] fraud. [There was] brutal and excessive force by police to suppress demonstrations, severely injuring at least 300 protesters, and killing at least one protester. Police arrested close to 1,000 people, including national leaders of the opposition, local opposition party members, activists from nongovernmental organizations, journalists, and election officials and observers who challenged the fraud. [There were] numerous cases of police torture—through severe beatings, electric shocks, and threats of male rape against opposition leaders, particularly by the Organized Crime Unit of the Ministry of Interior."

Across the Caspian Sea in Uzbekistan—yet another Central Asian country where oppressive leaders steal the nation's oil wealth while most people make do on $20 a month—anti-corruption activist Ruslan Sharipov currently languishes in prison under the Uzbek regime's trumped-up sodomy charges. "During the first days of his detention," says Human Rights Watch, "arresting officers threatened Sharipov with physical violence, including rape with a bottle."

Charming fellows, our allies in the war on terrorism.

JAN. 21, 2005

In neighboring Kazakhstan, independent journalist Lira Baiseitova published a story about Swiss bank accounts allegedly used by Kazakh dictator Nursultan Nazarbayev to funnel stolen oil revenues. The next day, her 25-year-old daughter Leila "disappeared." One month later, she turned up dead in police custody. Cops said she had tried to hang herself—a standard "cause" of death in Central Asian jails.

Admittedly, Central Asia spans four time zones. We'll need about a million troops to occupy the whole steppe, but what the heck—some analysts think the region will supply eighty percent of the world's oil in twenty-five years. It'll be worth it! Oh, and there's the liberation thing too.

Syria, Iran and Lebanon: add them to the list. All three nations jail and torture political opponents, censor journalists and threaten human rights organizers. Allow 75,000 troops for Syria and Lebanon, plus another half million for Iran, and let freedom ring.

While we're taking out oppressive Mediterranean regimes, both Israel and Yassir Arafat's Palestinian Authority have got to go. Israeli strongman Ariel Sharon, complicit in war crimes during the 1980s, is building a Berlin Wall-style "security fence" dividing Arab villages, employs child soldiers in his army and wants a law that would ban Palestinians married to Israelis from living in Israel. Meanwhile, Arafat treats public funds like his personal bank account, jails and tortures political opponents and stands by as his officials assassinate one another. To hell with the "road map"—both sides need an old-fashioned preemptive asswhupping, American-style! (Allow another 300,000 occupation soldiers.)

A couple of million troops here, a few trillion dollars there, pretty soon we'll have this whole Middle East thing all worked out.

Then: Across to Africa.

After that: South America Libre!

And don't forget: Eastern Europe—free at last!

Last Word

MARCH 2, 2004—Democrat or Republican, rich or poor, black or white, Americans think of themselves as culturally and politically centrist. In a survey conducted every year since the end of Vietnam, the Harris Poll consistently finds that more Americans call themselves "moderate" than liberal or conservative. And both liberals and conservatives consider themselves less extreme than those on the other side of the ideological fence. *E pluribus moderatus nihil.*

The 2004 campaign is shaping up as a clash of the more-moderate-than-thous.

Senator John Kerry was perceived as the most electable Democrat this year because he seemed more moderate than his rivals. That worries Republicans. "Bush's strategists," reports *USA Today*, "want to negate Kerry's self-portrait of a moderate."

Machiavellian consultant Dick Morris is urging GOP honchos to invest some of their $200 million campaign war chest into Willie Horton-style attack ads depicting Kerry as "an ultra liberal extremist." Kerry, hoping that his weaseling on Iraq and gay marriage will cause voters to perceive him as a moderate, accuses Bush of running "an extreme radical adminis-tration." Look for more of the same in the weeks and months to come.

Americans love the crassest forms of mass entertainment the human mind can conjure up: wrestling, football, midget-dating reality shows. Their spectator sports are extreme, yet they elect men who, though they acknowledge that those in power have messed everything up, pledge to change just about nothing. We believe that our presidents should be calm, reserved and, yeah, "moderate." Happy-go-lucky dudes like Dennis Kucinich and angry hell-raisers like Dean are fun for bar-hopping, fronting punk bands and flirting with during pri-mary season, but we worry about what such wild cards might do in the Oval Office. That the president should be our national dad is a radically stupid premise.

At any given time, we face a wide variety of problems and challenges. Certainly, many of these matters call for a calm, reasoned approach—you don't triple interest rates at the first sign of inflation or ban imports because free trade is causing corporations to move jobs over-seas. Other issues— the long-term, seemingly intractable afflictions that seem to go on for-ever—may require radical solutions.

More than 100 million people are un- or underinsured. But John Kerry's proposal would cover a mere 27 million citizens and Bush's plan is even more modest, covering only the 10 million workers who are unemployed. Nothing short of a radical healthcare plan, one that provides every American with free or affordable access to medical attention, will solve the problem.

Like Bill Clinton before him, Kerry approaches contentious issues with self-contradic-tion rather than bona fide moderation. Voting for the invasion on Iraq while standing against

the funding of the occupation, for example, couples a radical right-wing stance—preemptive warfare—with an equally radical, liberal opposition to neoimperialism. These conflicting votes exacerbate two equally problematic positions without solving either.

Democrats assert that the current administration is the most radical in U.S. history. They're right, and their argument may persuade some swing voters come November. But the mere fact that Bush's approach to foreign and domestic policy appears extreme doesn't intrinsically make him dangerous. A more moderate response to the 9/11 attacks—firing a few Cruise missiles à la Clinton or freezing some bank accounts—would have fallen woefully short of what was called for. The problem with the Bush Administration is that its focus was completely wrongheaded: going after Afghanistan instead of Pakistan, Iraq instead of Saudi Arabia, spying on Americans instead of improving airline security, blaming cave-dwelling "evildoers" rather than reexamining longstanding U.S. relationships with hated puppet regimes. Their actions created new problems while those related to 9/11 remain unaddressed.

That's the intrinsic problem with radicalism: When you're wrong, you're really wrong. That's why you have to be careful.

Should Kerry prevail in the general election, radical solutions will be required to fix Bush's radical mistakes. To stem the bleeding of men and treasure in Iraq and Afghanistan, he'll need to withdraw our forces as quickly as possible. To get the federal budget back on track, he'll have to eliminate Bush's tax cuts. To restore our international reputation, he'll be forced to release the Guantánamo and other detainees, and apologize to the world for our post-9/11 excesses. Anything less—anything moderate—would be too radical to contemplate.

Ted Rall
New York City